COLOUR GU
SPRING WILD
OF WESTERN AUSTRALIA
Part 2
Perth and the Southwest

CW00740016

Eddy Wajon

WAJON PUBLISHING COMPANY
2000

Books in the series

Colour Guide to Spring Wildflowers of Western Australia

Part 1:   Kalbarri and the Goldfields (1999)
Part 2:   Perth and the Southwest (2000)
Part 3:   Esperance and the Wheatbelt (2001)

Text and photographs copyright © Johannes Edmund Wajon 2000

ISBN 0 9577817 0 9

First published in 2000
Wajon Publishing Company
16 Eckersley Heights, Winthrop, Western Australia 6150
Phone +61-8-9310-2936
e-mail: wajonpub@wantree.com.au

Designed by Rebecca Machin, Donna Wajon and Lisa Brown
Typeset by Keystrokes Digital Prepress Bureau, Perth, Western Australia
Printed and bound by Kyodo Printing Company, Singapore

This book is dedicated to my wife, Donna. Thank you for your patience while I wa taking all the photographs, your assistance in typing, and for your encouragement i finally producing the book after taking photos for so many years.

I would like to thank the Department of Conservation and Land Management c Western Australia for use of the Reference Herbarium and the FloraBase database. would also like to thank Herbarium staff for assistance with identification, and Su Patrick and Alex George for technical review.

Cover photograph: Blue Leschenaultia and Yellow Buttercups
Photographs on contents page (top to bottom): Gillam's Bell, Magnificent Coneflowe Showy Dryandra, Beautiful Yellow Pea, Hidden Featherflower, Bird Orchid, Blu Leschenaultia.

CONTENTS

Map of Western Australia iv

Index to map of Western Australia v

Map of Perth and the Southwest vi

Index to map of Perth and the Southwest vii

Flora roads vii

How to use this book viii

The Flowers 1

Red flowers	1
Pink and mauve flowers	19
Orange and brown flowers	39
Yellow flowers	53
White flowers	73
Green and black flowers	93
Blue and purple flowers	95

List of multi-coloured wildflowers 113

Index 116

Selected reading 120

iv

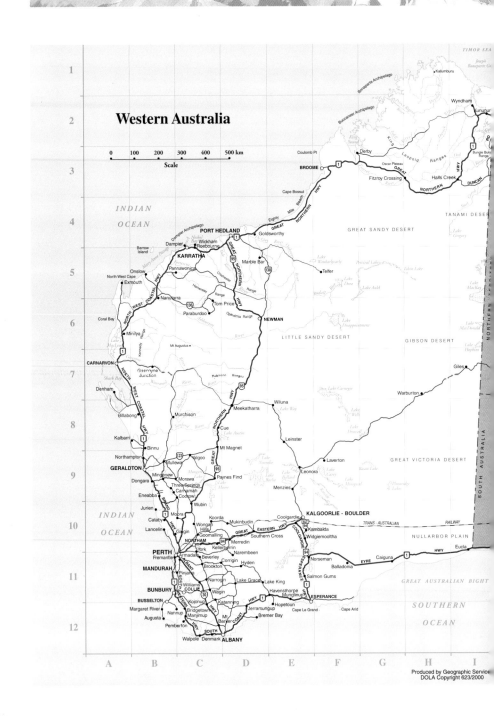

Western Australia

0   100   200   300   400   500 km

Scale

Produced by Geographic Service
DOLA Copyright 623/2000

Index to map of Western Australia

lbany	D12	Giles	I7	Mullewa	B9
rmadale	C11	Gingin	B10	Munglinup	E11
ugusta	B12	Goomalling	C10	Murchison	B8
alladonia	F11	Hopetoun	E12	Nannup	B12
everley	C11	Hyden	D11	Nanutarra	B5
llabong	B8	Jerramungup	D12	Narembeen	D11
innu	B8	Jurien	B10	Narrogin	C11
emer Bay	D12	Kalbarri	B8	Newman	D6
ridgetown	C12	Kambalda	E10	Norseman	E11
ookton	C11	Kalgoorlie	E10	Northam	C10
roome	F3	Karratha	C5	Northampton	B9
unbury	B11	Katanning	C11	Onslow	B5
usselton	B12	Kellerberrin	C10	Paraburdoo	C6
aiguna	G11	Kojonup	C12	Paynes Find	C9
ape Arid	F12	Koorda	C10	Pemberton	C12
ape Le Grand	F12	Lake Grace	D11	Perth	C11
arnamah	B9	Lake King	D11	Pinjarra	C11
arnarvon	A7	Lancelin	B10	Port Hedland	D4
ataby	B10	Laverton	F9	Ravensthorpe	E11
ollie	C11	Leinster	E8	Salmon Gums	E11
oolgardie	E10	Leonora	E9	Shark Bay	A7
oorow	C9	Mandurah	B11	Southern Cross	D10
oral Bay	A6	Manjimup	C12	Three Springs	B9
orrigin	C11	Marble Bar	D5	Wagin	C11
ue	C8	Margaret River	B12	Walpole	C12
ampier	C4	Meekatharra	D8	Warburton	H7
enham	A7	Menzies	E9	Williams	C11
enmark	C12	Merredin	D10	Wiluna	E8
ongara	B9	Mingenew	B9	Wongan Hills	C10
eabba	B9	Minilya	A6	Wubin	C10
perance	E12	Moora	C10	Wyndham	I2
cla	I10	Morawa	B9	Yalgoo	C9
xmouth	A5	Mt Barker	C12	York	C10
ascoyne Junction	B7	Mt Magnet	C8		
eraldton	B9	Mukinbudin	D10		

Map of Perth and the Southwest

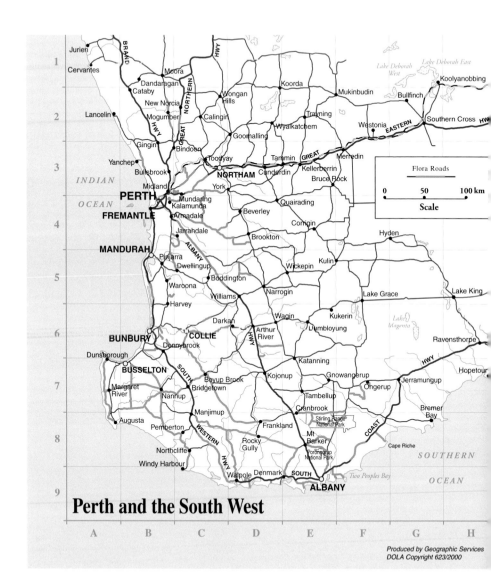

Perth and the South West

Index to map of Perth and the Southwest

TOWNS

Albany	E9	Goomalling	D2	Narrogin	D5
Armadale	B4	Harvey	B5	New Norcia	C2
Arthur River	D6	Hopetoun	H7	Northam	C3
Augusta	A8	Hyden	G4	Ongerup	F7
Beverley	D4	Jarrahdale	C4	Pemberton	C8
Bindoon	C3	Jerramungup	G7	Perth	B3
Boddington	C5	Jurien	A1	Pinjarra	B5
Boyup Brook	C7	Kalamunda	B4	Porongurup Range	E8
Bremer Bay	G8	Katanning	E7	Quairading	D4
Bridgetown	C7	Kellerberrin	E3	Rocky Gully	D8
Brookton	D4	Kojonup	D7	Southern Cross	G2
Bruce Rock	E3	Koorda	D2	Stirling Range	E8
Bullsbrook	B3	Kukerin	E6	Tammin	E3
Bunbury	B6	Kulin	F5	Toodyay	C3
Busselton	B7	Lake Grace	F5	Trayning	E2
Calingiri	C2	Lake King	H5	Two Peoples Bay	F9
Cape Riche	F8	Lancelin	A2	Wagin	D6
Collie	C6	Mandurah	B5	Walpole	D9
Corrigin	E4	Manjimup	C8	Waroona	B5
Cranbrook	E8	Margaret River	A7	Westonia	F2
Cunderdin	D3	Merredin	F3	Wickepin	E5
Darkan	D6	Midland	B3	Williams	D5
Denmark	E9	Mogumber	B2	Windy Harbour	C9
Donnybrook	B6	Moora	B1	Wongan Hills	C2
Dunsborough	A7	Mount Barker	E8	Wyakcatchem	D2
Frankland	D8	Mukinbudin	F2	Yanchep	B3
Gingin	B3	Mundaring	C3	York	D3
Gnowangerup	E7	Nannup	B7		

MAJOR ROADS

Gt. Northern H'way, New Norcia	C2	Tomingley Rd, Dryandra	D5	Boyup Brook-Cranbrook Rd	C7
Midlands Rd, Mogumber	B2	Henty Brook Rd, Burekup	B6	Frankland-Cranbrook Rd	D8
Wanneroo Rd, Yanchep	B3	Crooked Brook Rd, Dardanup	B6	Muirs H'way, Manjimup	C8–D8
Bindoon-Dewars Pool Rd	C3	Wellington-Lowden Rd, Dardanup	B6	South Coast H'way, Walpole	D9
Forty One Mile Rd, Toodyay	C3	Gavin Gully Rd, Donnybrook	B6	Thomson Rd, Walpole	D8–D9
Toodyay Rd	C3	Williams-Collie Rd	C6	Valley of the Giants Rd, Walpole	D9
Gt. Eastern H'way, Chidlow	C3	Coalfields Rd, Collie	C6	Peaceful Bay Rd	D9
Gt. Southern H'way, York	C3	Collie-Preston Rd	C6	Lower Denmark Rd, Albany	E9
John Forrest National Park Drv	C3	Donnybrook-Boyup Brook Rd	C6–C7	Cosy Corner Rd, Albany	E9
Zig-Zag, Gooseberry Hill	C4	Robinson Rd, Woodanilling	D6	Toompup Rd, Ongerup	F7
Mundaring Weir Rd, Kalamunda	C4	Crapella Rd, Kojonup	D6	Ongerup-Boxwood Hill Rd	F7
Brookton H'way	C4	Caves Rd, Margaret River	A7	Nightwell Rd, Borden	F7
Narra Rd, Dale	C4	Meelup Beach Rd, Dunsborough	A6	Chester Pass Rd, Amelup	F8
Albany H'way, Nth Bannister	C4–C5	Carters Rd, Margaret River	A7	Stirling Range Drv	E8
Halls Rd, Serpentine	B4	Vasse H'way, Nannup	B7–B8	Salt River Rd, Cranbrook	E8
Koyagin Rd, Brookton	D4	Sues Rd, Busselton	B7	Woongenilup Rd, Mt Barker	E8
Del Park Rd, North Dandalup	B5	Mowen Rd, Nannup	B7	Mt Barker-Porongurup Rd	E8
Old Coast Rd, Lake Clifton	B5	Brockman H'way, Nannup	B7–C7	Mt Barker-Denmark Rd	E8–E9
Wanga Brook Rd, Waroona	B5	Stewart Rd, Pemberton	B8	Nanarup Rd, Albany	E9
Logue Brook Dam Rd, Harvey	B5	Pemberton-Northcliffe Rd	C8	Two Peoples Bay Rd	F9
York-Williams Rd	D5	Windy Harbour Rd	C8	Sandalwood Rd, Cape Riche	F8
Wandering-Narrogin Rd	D5	South Western H'way, Manjimup	C8	South Coast H'way, Wellstead	F8

How to use this book

Western Australia has more than 12,000 species of flowering plants, making it one of the most botanically diverse areas in the world. Many of these grow in the south west of Western Australia. This guide contains photographs of 224 of the most common (and some not so common) wildflowers which can be found from July to November in the area between Perth, Augusta, Albany and Northam. Many of these wildflowers are also found in areas as far apart as Kalbarri, Hyden and Esperance. You will also see other wildflowers that are not shown in this book. Some of these may be shown in Parts 1 and 3 of this series, which cover Kalbarri and the Goldfields, and Esperance and the Wheatbelt respectively.

The wildflowers in this book are grouped by colour. The sequence of colours is that of the colours of the rainbow, i.e. red, orange, yellow, green and blue. Pink flowers follow the red flowers and white flowers follow the yellow flowers. Mauve flowers are included with pink, brown flowers are included with orange, cream flowers are included with white, black flowers are included with green, and purple or lilac flowers are included with blue. There is a strip of colour on the edge of each page which identifies the colour section. Some flowers are multi-coloured; other flowers may come in a variety of colours. Only one colour form is shown, but other colour forms are cross-referenced in the index. Multi-coloured flowers are placed in the section of the most obvious colour.

Within each colour section, the flowers are arranged approximately alphabetically by scientific name. A common name is given for each plant. Most of these common names are derived from the book "Common and Aboriginal Names of Western Australian Plant Species" by E.M. Bennett. The time of flowering, and how common the plant is, are indicated. How common the plant is refers to how abundant it is in the places where it grows. Very common means that many plants are present in an area and it should be very easy to find. The distribution of the plant is indicated by the main towns which bound the area where it may be found. The distribution indicates where the plant may be found, but it may not be present everywhere within that area. Where a plant grows is controlled by many factors including habitat and soil type. This is indicated in the text. All towns are shown in the maps at the front of the book. The maps also show main roads along which to see a good wildflower display.

When you find a wildflower, turn to the relevant colour section and scan the photographs for a flower that looks similar. Compare the real wildflower with the photograph. Read the description which describes the flower and plant in very simple terms. Note the size and shape of the leaves, and where the plant grows. If it does not seem to fit the description, look in the list of multi-coloured flowers because your plant may be shown in another colour section. Look at the list under the colour of the plant you are trying to identify, and turn to the photos of the flowers on the pages indicated. If you vaguely know the name of the plant, you might try going to the index of common or scientific names. As a last resort, look in the books in Part 1 or 3 of this series.

DATE	PLACE

LY–DECEMBER
OMMON

orest. Toodyay to Perth, Augusta and
annup.
hrub 0.2–1 m tall. Many bright red
airy flowers 2–3 cm long. Spear-shaped
aves 5–10 cm long x 10 mm wide.

HAIRY JUG FLOWER

Adenanthos barbiger

DATE	PLACE

CTOBER–JULY
OMMON

BASKET FLOWER

Adenanthos obovatus

orest and heath on sand and gravel. Perth to Augusta, Cape Riche, Ongerup and
arrogin.
hrub 0.3–1.5 m tall. Many bright red to orange flowers 2–3 cm long. Thick, flat round
spoon-shaped smooth leaves 1–2 cm long.

DATE	PLACE

MANGLES KANGAROO PAW

Anigozanthos manglesii subsp. *manglesii*

JULY–DECEMBER
VERY COMMON

Woodland and heath in sand. Gingin to Augusta, Rocky Gully, Katanning and Toodya
Herb 0.2–1.25 m tall. Group of eight to ten woolly red and green flowers 6–10 cm lon
on woolly red stems 1.25 m long. Flat, sword-shaped leaves 50–80 cm long x 1–2 cr
wide, mostly at base of plant. Subsp. *quadrans* common near Kalbarri has more red o
flower.

DATE	PLACE

RIGID CRANBERRY

Astroloma epacridis

JANUARY–DECEMBER
COMMON

Woodland in gravel. Dongara to Pinjarra, Albany, Cape Arid and Hyden.
Straggly shrub 0.1–1 m tall. Smooth red, pink or white flowers 1 cm long with wool
tips. Thick, shiny to rough, spear-shaped leaves 5–10 mm long x 1–3 mm wide, endin
in a sharp point.

DATE	PLACE

…1AY–JANUARY
…ERY COMMON

…/oodland and heath in sand. Cranbrook
…) Denmark and Esperance.
…nrub or tree 1–8 m tall. Red or orange
…owers with white woolly centres (woolly
…rown in bud) in a cylinder 5–10 cm
…ng x 8–10 cm wide. Prickly, wavy, saw-
…)othed leaves 3–10 cm long x 2–5 cm
…ide.

SCARLET BANKSIA
Banksia coccinea

DATE	PLACE

…:BRUARY–OCTOBER
…ERY COMMON

FIREWOOD BANKSIA
Banksia menziesii

…)rest and woodland in sand. Kalbarri to Mandurah, York and Three Springs.
…nrub or tree 1.5–7 m tall. Red or pink and orange or yellow flowers in a cylinder
…-15 cm long x 8–10 cm wide. Prickly, saw-toothed leaves 10–25 cm long x 1–4 cm wide.

DATE	PLACE

BARRENS BOTTLEBRUSH
Beaufortia anisandra

SEPTEMBER–JULY
COMMON

Woodland and heath in rock or sand. Cranbrook to Denmark and Hopetoun.
Shrub 0.2–1.5 m tall. Red to purple bottlebrush flowers in head 3–4 cm wide and 2 cm
high at end of branches. Crowded, round to oval, cupped leaves 10 mm long x 5 mm wide.

DATE	PLACE

STIRLING RANGE BOTTLEBRUSH
Beaufortia cyrtodonta

AUGUST–DECEMBER
VERY COMMON

Woodland and heath in sand or gravel. Cataby to Albany, Cape Arid and Lake Grace.
Shrub 0.25–1.5 m tall. Red bottlebrush flowers in groups 3–10 cm long and 2 cm high
along branches. Crowded, pointed, straight, flat, sometimes hairy, leaves 5–10 mm
long x 1 mm wide, usually in bunches along branches.

DATE	PLACE

GREY-LEAVED BOTTLEBRUSH

Beaufortia incana

UGUST–DECEMBER
NCOMMON

/oodland in gravel. Northam to Katanning, Lake Grace and Quairading.
¬rub 0.5–2 m tall. Red bottlebrush flowers in groups 3–10 cm long and 2 cm high
ong branches. Crowded, straight, silky, hairy, greyish leaves 5–10 mm long x 2 mm
⸱ide in bunches along branches.

DATE	PLACE

ALBANY BOTTLEBRUSH

Callistemon glaucus

EPTEMBER–DECEMBER
NCOMMON

/oodland and swamps. Busselton to Augusta, Albany and Collie.
¬rub 1–3 m tall. Red flowers in a cylinder 10–15 cm long x 6–7 cm wide at end of
⸱ranches. Spear-shaped leaves 5–15 cm long x 10–15 mm wide.

CAROUSEL SPIDER ORCHID
Caladenia arenicola

DATE	PLACE

AUGUST–OCTOBER
VERY COMMON

Woodland in sand. Lancelin to Perth an
Mandurah.
Slender plant 30–60 cm tall. One t
three salmon-red flowers 8–10 cm long
6–8 cm wide with long fringes on lip
Grass-like leaf 15–25 cm long x 5–10 mm
wide at base of plant.

COMMON DRAGON ORCHID
Caladenia barbarossa

DATE	PLACE

SEPTEMBER–NOVEMBER
VERY COMMON

Swamps, granite outcrops and sheoa
forests. Perth to Collie, Mount Barke
Esperance and Hyden.
Slender plant 10–30 cm tall. Red-stripe
yellow and green flower 2–4 cm long
2–3 cm wide with furry purple lip. Grass
like leaf 5 cm long x 5–10 mm wide a
base of plant.

DATE	PLACE

JGUST–OCTOBER
OMMON

BEE ORCHID
Caladenia discoidea

rest, woodland and heath. Kalbarri to Busselton, Mount Barker, Lake King, Esperance
d Narrogin.
ender plant 10–45 cm tall. One to four red and yellow-green flowers 2–3 cm long x
-3 cm wide with red lumps and long fringes on lip. Grass-like leaf 10–20 cm long x
) mm wide at base of plant.

DATE	PLACE

PTEMBER–OCTOBER
NCOMMON

rest and swamps. Perth to Augusta
d Albany.
ender plant 20–60 cm tall. One to three
ddish-brown flowers 6–8 cm long x 5 cm
de with long fringes and red tip to
hite lip, and thickened orange tips to
ree petals. Grass-like leaf 10–20 cm
ng x 5–15 mm wide at base of plant.

RUSTY SPIDER ORCHID
Caladenia ferruginea

BUTTERFLY ORCHID
Caladenia lobata

DATE	PLACE

SEPTEMBER–NOVEMBER
UNCOMMON

Forest. Busselton to Manjimup, Albar
and Stirling Range.
Slender plant 30–50 cm tall. One or tw
red, yellow and green flowers 8–10 c
long x 10 cm wide with long fringes ar
red tip to yellow lip. Grass-like leaf 10–20 c
long and 10 mm wide at base of plant

KING SPIDER ORCHID
Caladenia pectinata

DATE	PLACE

SEPTEMBER–OCTOBER
COMMON

Woodland and forest. Lancelin to Pert
Busselton, Albany, Bremer Bay and Ongeru
Slender plant 35–70 cm tall. One to thr
red and yellowish-green flowers 6–10 c
long x 6–7 cm wide with long fringes d
red and white lip and thickened yello
tips to three petals. Grass-like leaf 15–30 c
long x 2 cm wide at base of plant.

DATE	PLACE

EPTEMBER–OCTOBER
NCOMMON

CRAB-LIPPED SPIDER ORCHID
Caladenia plicata

Woodland. Busselton to Walpole, Albany, Hopetoun and Katanning.
Slender plant 20–35 cm tall. One to two red and yellow flowers 5 cm long x 3 cm wide with red lumps and long fringe on lip. Grass-like leaf 10–20 cm long and 10 mm wide at base of plant.

DATE	PLACE

EPTEMBER–DECEMBER
NCOMMON

SCARLET FLAME PEA
Chorizema rhombeum

Forest, woodland and coastal areas. Perth to Augusta, Cape Le Grand, Stirling Range and Boyup Brook.
Straggly or prostrate shrub 10–50 cm tall. Red to pink or orange and yellow pea flowers 10–25 mm across in groups near ends of branches. Oval to spear-shaped leaves 10–40 mm long x 5–10 mm wide, ending in a sharp point.

DATE	PLACE

MOUSE EARS

Calothamnus rupestris

JULY–NOVEMBER
COMMON

Forest in creeks or on granite outcrops. Perth to Armadale, Brookton and York.
Shrub 1–4 m tall. Red to pink flowers 3–4 cm long with hairy grey base in a bunch o
one side of branch. Crowded, needle-like leaves 1–3 cm long x 1 mm wide, ending i
a sharp point.

DATE	PLACE

FLAT ONE-SIDED BOTTLEBRUSH

Calothamnus torulosus

AUGUST–NOVEMBER
UNCOMMON

Forest and heath in sand or on granite outcrops. Eneabba to Armadale, Jarrahdale an
Coorow.
Shrub 10–60 cm tall. Red to green flowers 2.5–3 cm long with hairy white base aroun
one side of branch. Crowded, needle-like leaves 2–6 cm long x 1 mm wide.

DATE	PLACE

MAY–JUNE, AUGUST–NOVEMBER
UNCOMMON

Heath. Rocky hillsides and gullies of Stirling Range and Porongurup Range. Shrub 0.5–2 m tall. Hanging red-and-white tubular bell-shaped flowers 3–4 cm long x 1–3 cm wide. Thick, slightly folded, oblong-elliptical leaves 1–2 cm long x 2–5 mm wide.

MONDURUP BELL
Darwinia macrostegia

DATE	PLACE

AUGUST–NOVEMBER
UNCOMMON

CRANBROOK BELL
Darwinia meeboldii

Woodland. Rocky areas at Cranbrook and western end of Stirling Range. Shrub 0.5–3 m tall. Hanging white to green bell-shaped flowers with red tips 3–4 cm long x 3 cm wide. Crowded, pointed, straight leaves 1 cm long x 2 mm wide.

DATE	PLACE

AUGUST–NOVEMBER
COMMON

Heath. Rocky hillsides at western end o
Stirling Range.
Shrub 0.5–2 m tall. Hanging red bell
shaped flowers 2–3 cm long x 2 cm
wide. Crowded straight leaves 5–10 mm
long x 2 mm wide.

GILLAM'S BELL

Darwinia oxylepis

DATE	PLACE

SEPTEMBER–DECEMBER
UNCOMMON

WITTWERS MOUNTAIN BELL

Darwinia wittwerorum

Woodland in clay. Central area of Stirling Range.
Shrub 0.3–1.5 m tall. Hanging red-and-white ball-shaped flowers 2 cm long x 2 cm
wide. Crowded straight leaves 5–10 mm long x 1 mm wide.

DATE	PLACE

)CTOBER–NOVEMBER
COMMON

Heath. Peaks of Stirling Range.
Shrub 0.5–1 m tall. Hanging red to
orange tubular flowers 2–3 cm long x
0.5–1.5 cm wide. Broad straight leaves
–2 cm long x 2–4 mm wide.

TOOLBRUNUP BELL
Darwinia hypericifolia

DATE	PLACE

MAY–FEBRUARY
UNCOMMON

wamps. Augusta to Albany, Esperance
nd Rocky Gully.
Shrub 0.5–2.5 m tall. Single usually
anging red to pink flower 10–15 mm
ong x 5 mm wide at the end of short
de branches. Twisted leaves 0.5–2.5 cm
ong x 2–5 mm wide, ending in a sharp
oint.

SPINDLE HEATH
Cosmelia rubra

DATE	PLACE

SOUTHERN ROSE

Diplolaena dampieri

JULY–NOVEMBER
COMMON

Coastal limestone and dunes and granite rocks. Perth to Augusta.
Shrub 0.5–2 m tall. Hanging hairy red to orange flowers 15–25 mm across with furry triangular green leaf-like covers 10–20 mm long. Oblong to elliptical leaves 15–45 mm long x 5–15 mm wide, smooth and bright green above, furry and dull green below.

DATE	PLACE

GRANITE ROSE

Diplolaena graniticola

JULY–DECEMBER
UNCOMMON

Woodland on granite rocks. Mundaring to Collie, Bridgetown, Wagin and York.
Shrub 1–1.5 m tall. Hanging hairy red or yellow flowers 15–25 mm across with furry triangular green leaf-like covers 10–15 mm long. Soft, furry elliptical leaves 15–30 mm long x 1–2 cm wide.

DATE	PLACE

AUGUST–DECEMBER
COMMON

CRINKLE-LEAVED POISON
Gastrolobium villosum

orest in gravel. Cataby to Perth, Frankland, York and New Norcia.
rostrate or spreading shrub 0.1–1 m tall. Red to pink or orange pea flowers 10 mm
cross in spike 10–20 cm long, some distance from the leaves. Wavy, sometimes prickly,
val or round leaves 2–5 cm long x 1–3 cm wide.

DATE	PLACE

EPTEMBER–JULY
OMMON

WILSON'S GREVILLEA
Grevillea wilsonii

orest in gravel or sand. Toodyay to Perth, Harvey and Boddington.
hrub 0.5–1 m tall. Many red flowers in head 5–8 cm long. Leaves 3–6 cm long,
ivided into many sharp needle-like leaflets 5–25 mm long x 1 mm wide.

DATE	PLACE

SCARLET RUNNER
Kennedia prostrata

MAY–NOVEMBER
VERY COMMON

Forest and woodland in sand or gravel. Shark Bay to Perth, Dunsborough, Albany, Esperance and Southern Cross.
Prostrate vine with stems 1–2 m long. Red and yellow pea flowers 2–3 cm across. Wavy, crinkled, oval or round leaves 1–6 cm long x 1–4 cm wide.

DATE	PLACE

AUGUST–OCTOBER
UNCOMMON

RED MARIANTHUS
Marianthus erubescens

Woodland in sand, clay or gravel. Mingenew to Eneabba, Lancelin, Denmark, Albany and Westonia.
Climbing vine 1–4 m tall with red stems. Red tubular flowers 2 cm long. Shiny, oval or spear-shaped leaves 2–4 cm long x 1–2 cm wide.

DATE	PLACE

EPTEMBER–APRIL
NCOMMON

ROBIN REDBREAST BUSH
Melaleuca lateritia

dges of swamps in sand. Kalbarri to Perth, Augusta, Albany and Boyup Brook.
hrub 2–4 m tall. Red to orange flowers in a cylinder 4–10 cm long x 3–5 cm wide.
pear-shaped leaves 1–2 cm long x 1 mm wide.

DATE	PLACE

UGUST–OCTOBER
ERY COMMON

RED BEAKS
Pyrorchis nigricans

orest and woodland usually only after fire. Kalbarri to Augusta, Albany, Esperance and
outhern Cross.
ender plant 5–30 cm tall. Two to eight red and white flowers 2–3 cm long and
–3 cm wide. Heart-shaped leaf 2–15 cm long x 3–8 cm wide at base of plant.

DATE	PLACE

HAIRY RED PEA

Nemcia leakeana

JULY–NOVEMBER
UNCOMMON

Heath in rocky soil. Stirling Range.
Shrub 1–2 m tall. Red to orange pea flowers (woolly white in bud) 20 mm across i
clusters along branches. Oval to elliptical leaves 3–6 cm long x 2–4 cm wide, ending i
a small point.

DATE	PLACE

MOUNTAIN PEA

Nemcia rubra

AUGUST–NOVEMBER
COMMON

Heath in rocky soil. Peaks of Stirling Range.
Shrub 1–1.5 m tall. Hanging red to purple or orange pea flowers (woolly brown-whit
in bud) 2–3 cm long x 10 mm wide in clusters along branches. Oval to elliptical leave
3–8 cm long x 2–3 cm wide, ending in a small point, often in groups of 3 along branch

DATE	PLACE

:PTEMBER–DECEMBER
OMMON

'oodland and heath in wet areas.
ranbrook to Albany, Bremer Bay and
rramungup.
nrub 25–60 cm high. Round pink and
hite flowers 1–4 cm across. Crowded,
raight, pointed leaves 2–5 mm long x
5 mm wide.

ALBANY DAISY
Actinodium calocephalum

DATE	PLACE

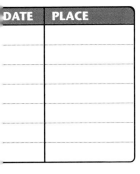

JGUST–OCTOBER
:RY COMMON

>rest and woodland in sand. Kalbarri to
ugusta, Albany, Esperance and Lake
race.
ender plant 20–45 cm tall. One to four
nk flowers 4 cm long x 3 cm wide with
ort fringes on pink and white lip.
rass-like leaf 10–25 cm long x 15–30 mm
ide at base of plant.

PINK FAIRIES
Caladenia latifolia

FOXTAILS

Andersonia caerulea

DATE	PLACE

ALL YEAR
UNCOMMON

Forest and heath in sand. Brookton t
Bunbury, Denmark, Albany, Munglinu
and Bruce Rock .
Straggly or upright shrub 0.3–1 m tal
Numerous bearded pink and blue flowe
5–10 mm long in spike at the end o
branches. Twisted leaves 2–15 mm long
2–3 mm wide, ending in a sharp point.

SPIKED ANDERSONIA

Andersonia simplex

DATE	PLACE

MARCH–JANUARY
COMMON

Heath in sand or gravel. Mount Barker t
Walpole, Bremer Bay and Cranbrook.
Shrub 0.1–1.2 m high. Group of pink o
red and blue flowers 5 mm long in
spike at the end of branches. Twiste
leaves 2–15 mm long x 2 mm wide
ending in a sharp point.

DATE	PLACE

JGUST–JANUARY
NCOMMON

rest and woodland in gravel. Armadale
Augusta, Albany and Kojonup.
rub 0.2–2 m tall. Pink, blue or purple
wers 15–20 mm across in clusters at
d of branches. Spear-shaped leaves
-2 cm long x 2–5 mm wide.

BUSHY BORONIA
Boronia fastigiata

DATE	PLACE

JGUST–OCTOBER
JMMON

PINK BORONIA
Boronia pulchella

odland and forest in sand. Stirling Range.
rub 0.5–1 m tall. Pink flowers 15–20 mm across in clusters at end of branches. Leaves
4 cm long in 5–15 pairs of straight leaflets 5–10 mm long x 1–2 mm wide along leaf.

DATE	PLACE

STICKY STARFLOWER

Calytrix glutinosa

AUGUST–NOVEMBER
COMMON

Heath on rock. Northampton to Harvey, Wyalkatchem, Wubin and Mullewa.
Shrub 0.2–1 m tall. Sticky pink star flowers with white centres 2 cm across and hairy pink tails. Straight, three-sided leaves 5–10 mm long x 1 mm wide.

DATE	PLACE

SEPTEMBER–JULY
COMMON

Forest and woodland. Gingin to Perth, Augusta, Cape Le Grand and Kojonup. Slender shrub 0.2–1.5 m tall. Pink purple pea-like flowers 5 mm long spike 5–10 cm long at end of branch. Thick, straight, pointed leaves 5–15 mm long x 1–2 mm wide with ridge on back.

COMMON MILKWORT

Comesperma virgatum

DATE	PLACE

JLY–JANUARY
OMMON

/oodland and heath in rocky soil.
:irling Range.
hrub 0.3–1.5 m tall. Hanging pink to
:d or white bell-shaped flowers 1.5–3 cm
ng x 2 cm wide. Crowded straight
aves 5–10 mm long x 1 mm wide.

COMMON MOUNTAIN BELL
Darwinia lejostyla

DATE	PLACE

JGUST–DECEMBER
:RY COMMON

>rest, woodland and heath. Shark Bay
 Augusta, Esperance, Balladonia and
mmin.
imbing plant 0.1–1 m tall with red
ems. Pink to red or white flowers 2–3 cm
:ross. Sticky, hairy, round leaves 5 mm
:ross in groups of three on stem.

PINK RAINBOW
Drosera menziesii

DATE	PLACE

PINK ENAMEL ORCHID

Elythranthera emarginata

OCTOBER–DECEMBER
COMMON

Woodland and heath. Kalbarri to Albany, Esperance and Merredin.
Slender plant 15–25 cm tall. One to four glossy pink flowers 3–5 cm across. Grass-like leaf 4–8 cm long x 7 mm wide at base of plant.

DATE	PLACE

HAIRY PINK PEA

Gompholobium villosum

OCTOBER–JANUARY
VERY COMMON

Forest and heath in sand. Busselton to Margaret River, Denmark, Bremer Bay and Stirling Range.
Shrub 0.5–2 m tall. Hairy pink to purple pea flowers 1–2 cm across in clusters at ends of branches. Masses of rough to hairy needle-like leaves 1–2 cm long x 1 mm wide.

DATE	PLACE

UGUST–OCTOBER
OMMON

orest and woodland in gravel. Perth to
ugusta, Albany, Manjimup and
rookton.
traggly shrub 1–3.5 m tall. Pink, white
r cream flowers in clusters 3–5 cm
cross. Prickly, wavy leaves 5–20 cm long
2–6 cm wide wrapped around stem.
ard, cylindrical woody nut 3 cm long x
cm wide with large beak at end.

PRICKLY HAKEA
Hakea amplexicaulis

DATE	PLACE

LL YEAR
ERY COMMON

SNAKEBUSH
Hemiandra pungens

orest, woodland and heath in sand. Kalbarri to Augusta, Bremer Bay, Wagin and Coorow.
ostrate or erect shrub 0.1–1 m tall. Slightly to very hairy pink, white or purple flowers
)–15 mm long x 5–10 mm wide. Spear-shaped leaves 5–10 mm long x 1–2 mm wide,
ghtly to very hairy, and ending in a sharp point.

DATE	PLACE

SILKY HEMIGENIA
Hemigenia incana

AUGUST–NOVEMBER
COMMON

Woodland and heath in sand and gravel. Jurien to Perth, Pemberton, Walpol Munglinup, Wickepin and Quairading.
Shrub 0.3–1.5 m tall. Hairy pink to blue, lilac or purple flowers 2 cm across. Thic velvety, hairy, oblong to oval leaves 1–5 cm long x 5–10 mm wide.

DATE	PLACE

JUNE–NOVEMBER
COMMON

Forest and woodland in sand and grave Northam to Perth, Augusta and Albany Shrub 0.5–1.5 m high. Pink to re flowers 10–15 mm across in spik 10–20 cm long along stem. Pointe spear-shaped leaves 10–20 mm long 1–2 mm wide.

SWAN RIVER MYRTLE
Hypocalymma robustum

DATE	PLACE

JNE–OCTOBER
COMMON

Voodland and heath in rock and gravel.
urien to Perth and Wongan Hills.
hrub 0.2–1 m tall. Pink or white flowers
–3 cm across in compressed spikes
–10 cm long along branch. Pointed
aves 10–25 mm long, some divided
nto three to five segments 5–10 mm
ong x 1 mm wide, in clusters along
ranch.

FLAT-TOPPED CONEFLOWER

Isopogon asper

DATE	PLACE

PRIL–OCTOBER
NCOMMON

eath in gravel. Cranbrook to Albany
nd Cape Riche.
hrub 0.5–1.5 m tall. Pink flowers in
ntidy, globular heads 2–4 cm across.
rickly, wedge- or fan-shaped or toothed
aves 2–5 cm long x 1–4 cm wide.

STIRLING RANGE CONEFLOWER

Isopogon baxteri

DATE	PLACE

JULY–OCTOBER
COMMON

Forest and woodland. Eneabba to Perth
Darkan and Wongan Hills.
Shrub 0.5–1.5 m tall. Pink flowers in
globular heads 3–6 cm across. Prickly
wavy leaves 3–6 cm long divided into
three spoon-shaped lobes 10–15 mm
long x 1–2 mm wide, usually ending in
sharp point.

PINCUSHION CONEFLOWER
Isopogon dubius

DATE	PLACE

JULY–DECEMBER
COMMON

ROSE CONEFLOWER
Isopogon formosus

Heath. Busselton to Augusta, Esperance and Rocky Gully.
Shrub 0.2–2 m tall. Pink flowers in globular heads 4–6 cm across. Leaves 2–4 cm long
divided into many sharp, pointed, needle-like sections 5–10 mm long x 1 mm wide.

DATE	PLACE

ːUGUST–NOVEMBER
ːNCOMMON

ːleath on slopes and peaks of mountains.
ːtirling Range.
ːhrub 1–3 m tall. Pink flowers in globular
ːeads 6–8 cm across. Broad, wavy,
ːointed, spear-shaped leaves 5–15 cm
ːong x 3–5 cm wide.

MAGNIFICENT CONEFLOWER
Isopogon latifolius

DATE	PLACE

ːUGUST–JANUARY
ːOMMON

ːorest and heath near swamps. Stirling
ːange to Denmark and Cape Riche.
ːlant 40–60 cm tall. Hanging pink
ːowers 15–25 mm long in spike 4–6 cm
ːong x 1–2 cm wide on a stalk 40–60 cm
ːong. Flat, oblong leaves 20–40 cm long
ː 1–2 mm wide, all at base of plant.

PINK HOODED LILY
Johnsonia teretifolia

DATE	PLACE

HAIRY KUNZEA

Kunzea preissiana

SEPTEMBER–NOVEMBER
VERY COMMON

Woodland and heath in sand or gravel. Brookton to Albany, Esperance and Corrigin.
Shrub 0.5–1.5 m tall. Masses of very hairy pink to purple globular flowers 10–15 mm
across at end of branches. Straight, oblong, often hairy leaves 5–10 mm long x 1–2 mm
wide.

DATE	PLACE

CURVED-LEAF KUNZEA

Kunzea recurva

AUGUST–NOVEMBER
COMMON

Woodland in gravel and rock. Waroona to Augusta, Albany, Esperance, Ongerup and
Boyup Brook.
Shrub 0.5–2 m tall. Pink or purple globular flowers 10–15 mm across. Round or oval
shaped leaves 2–5 mm long x 2–5 mm wide, curled back on stem.

DATE	PLACE

JULY–NOVEMBER
COMMON

Forest or woodland in wet areas. Perth to Augusta, Albany, Manjimup and Brookton. Shrub 0.5–4 m tall. Pink or red and white tubular flowers 5 mm long x 1 mm wide in spikes 5–10 cm long. Flat to wavy, veined, spear-shaped leaves 5–15 cm long and 1–2 cm wide, in a ring around stem.

TASSEL FLOWER
Leucopogon verticillatus

DATE	PLACE

JULY–NOVEMBER
COMMON

Woodland or heath on granite rocks or near streams. Kalbarri to Pinjarra, Kukerin, Munglinup, Norseman, Leonora and Murchison. Shrub 0.5–2.5 m tall. Pink to mauve or white globular flowers 10–15 mm across, opposite each other in spikes 5–10 cm long. Straight or elliptical leaves 10–50 mm long x 1 mm wide.

GRACEFUL HONEYMYRTLE
Melaleuca radula

DATE	PLACE

HOLLY-LEAVED MIRBELIA

Mirbelia dilatata

SEPTEMBER–DECEMBER
COMMON

Forest and woodland. New Norcia to Perth, Augusta, Esperance and Lake King.
Shrub 0.5–3 m tall. Pink, violet or purple pea flowers 15 mm across. Prickly, triangula
leaves 1–3 cm long x 1–2 cm wide divided into three to seven fingers, each ending ir
a sharp point.

DATE	PLACE

JUNE–NOVEMBER
VERY COMMON

Forest, woodland and heath in sand o
gravel. Eneabba to Augusta, Wind
Harbour and Toodyay.
Shrub 0.2–1 m high. Pink, mauve, whit
or blue flowers 1 cm across in a spik
5–20 cm long. Rough, straight leave
5–20 mm long x 1–2 mm wide.

PEPPER AND SALT

Philotheca spicata

DATE	PLACE

JLY–SEPTEMBER
ERY COMMON

orest and heath in gravel and rock.
1ogumber to Pinjarra and Toodyay.
hrub 0.5–2 m tall. Hairy pinkish-grey to
vhite flowers 15–25 mm across in a
pike 10–50 cm long x 5–8 cm across.
rickly leaves 2–4 cm long divided into
ve or nine oval lobes 5–20 mm long x
mm wide, each ending in a sharp point.

GRANITE PETROPHILE
Petrophile biloba

DATE	PLACE

EPTEMBER–DECEMBER
OMMON

PIXIE MOPS
Petrophile linearis

orest, woodland and heath in sand. Eneabba to Busselton, Augusta, Pemberton and
ollie.
hrub 0.2–1 m tall. Hairy pinkish-grey flowers in globular heads 4–5 cm across. Thick,
at, curved leaves 2–10 cm long x 2–5 mm wide.

DATE	PLACE

AUGUST–FEBRUARY
VERY COMMON

Heath in coastal sand dunes an
headlands. Dongara to Augusta an
Cape Arid.
Shrub 0.3–1.5 m tall. Pink flowers i
globular heads 2–3 cm across. Stiff, fla
glossy, oval leaves 5–10 mm long
3–5 mm wide, folded along the edge.

COASTAL BANJINE
Pimelea ferruginea

DATE	PLACE

SEPTEMBER–DECEMBER
VERY COMMON

Woodland and heath in sand and roc
near the coast. Yanchep to Augusta an
Two Peoples Bay.
Shrub 0.3–1 m tall. Pale to rose pink o
red-purple flowers in globular head
2–4 cm across. Soft, flat, not gloss
spear-shaped leaves 1–3 cm long
2–5 mm wide.

ROSE BANJINE
Pimelea rosea

DATE	PLACE

EPTEMBER–JANUARY
ERY COMMON

ROSE-TIPPED MULLA MULLA
Ptilotus manglesii

orest, woodland and heath in sand or gravel. Kalbarri to Busselton, Albany and Hyden.
rostrate herb with stems 5–60 cm long. Hairy, pink and white globular flowers 3–5 cm
cross. Straight or spoon-shaped leaves 2–10 cm long x 0.2–5 cm wide, mostly at base
f plant.

DATE	PLACE

UGUST–DECEMBER
NCOMMON

KARRI FANFLOWER
Scaevola auriculata

orest and woodland on hillsides. Pemberton to Walpole, Albany and Mount Barker.
hrub 0.1–1 m tall. Pink, mauve or blue flowers 10–15 mm across. Toothed circular,
val or oblong leaves 1–4 cm long x 2–20 mm wide, clasping stem.

PINK FOUNTAIN TRIGGERPLANT
Stylidium brunonianum

DATE	PLACE

SEPTEMBER–DECEMBER
COMMON

Forest, woodland and heath. Kalbarri t
Augusta, Albany and Ongerup.
Slender plant 10–60 cm tall. Pink, purpl
or white flowers 10–15 mm long an
5 mm wide in spike 2–15 cm long
Straight leaves 5–25 mm long x 1–2 mr
wide in rings around stem at base c
plant and along stem.

BOOK TRIGGERPLANT
Stylidium calcaratum

DATE	PLACE

AUGUST–DECEMBER
VERY COMMON

Forest, woodland and heath. Kalbarri t
Augusta, Esperance and Coolgardie.
Slender plant 2–20 cm tall. One or tw
pink or white flowers 5–10 mm long an
3–5 mm wide at end of stalk 5–10 cr
long. Oval leaves 2–5 mm long x 1–2 mr
wide in rings around stem at base c
plant.

DATE	PLACE

UGUST–MARCH
OMMON

CLIMBING TRIGGERPLANT

Stylidium scandens

orest, woodland and heath in swampy areas. Bunbury to Augusta, Bremer Bay and Manjimup.
Climbing plant 0.2–2 m tall. Pink flowers 10–15 mm long and 10 mm wide, on red stems. Straight or spear-shaped leaves 1–2 cm long x 1–2 mm wide, curled at end, in several rings around stem.

DATE	PLACE

EPTEMBER–NOVEMBER
OMMON

PINCUSHION TRIGGERPLANT

Stylidium uniflorum

Woodland and heath in sand or gravel. Quairading to Pinjarra, Albany and Bremer Bay.
ow plant in tufts 5–10 cm tall. Single pink, orange, yellow or white flower 10–15 mm ong and 3–5 mm wide at end of hairy stalk 5–10 cm long. Straight, toothed leaves 0–25 mm long x 1–2 mm wide, all at base of plant.

DATE	PLACE

AUGUST–DECEMBER
COMMON

Forest and heath in gravel. Geraldton t
Augusta, Cape Riche, Narrogin an
Moora.
Shrub 0.1–1 m tall. Hanging pink t
purple flowers 1–2 cm across. Hair
elliptical or oblong leaves 5–25 mm lon
x 1–10 mm wide on spiny stems.

BLACK-EYED SUSAN

Tetratheca hirsuta

DATE	PLACE

MAY–JANUARY
VERY COMMON

PINK PETTICOATS

Utricularia multifida

Swamps and rock pools. Eneabba to Augusta, Albany and Wickepin.
Herb 5–30 cm high. Pink flowers 10–15 mm across with large lower lip divided in
three lobes. Spoon-shaped leaves 5–10 mm long x 2 mm wide, all at base of plant.

DATE	PLACE

.PRIL–DECEMBER
OMMON

/oodland in sand or gravel. Kulin to
Valpole, Hopetoun and Ravensthorpe.
Creeping shrub with above-ground stem
0–50 cm high. Brown or orange woolly
owers in a cylinder 10–20 cm long x
–10 cm wide. Lobed or saw-toothed
aves 10–50 cm long x 2–6 cm wide.

PROSTRATE BANKSIA
Banksia gardneri

DATE	PLACE

JLY–APRIL
OMMON

NODDING BANKSIA
Banksia nutans

/oodland and heath in sand. Wagin to Albany and Esperance.
nrub 0.5–1.5 m high. Hanging brown, pink or purple flowers in a cylinder 4–8 cm
ng x 4–8 cm wide. Crowded, straight, pointed leaves 1–2 cm long x 1–2 mm wide.

DATE	PLACE

CREEPING BANKSIA
Banksia repens

SEPTEMBER–NOVEMBER
COMMON

Heath in sand. Cranbrook to Albany and Cape Arid.
Creeping shrub with underground stem 30–50 cm high. Brown to yellow, orange o
pinkish woolly flowers in a cylinder 10–15 cm long x 6–10 cm wide some distance fro
leaves. Large, wavy leaves 20–50 cm long x 5–20 cm wide divided into toothed finge
2–10 cm long x 5–15 mm wide.

DATE	PLACE

SEPTEMBER–NOVEMBER
UNCOMMON

Woodland and heath in rock or san
Stirling Range.
Shrub or tree 0.5–4 m high. Brown
purple woolly flowers in a cylinder 5–15 c
long x 5–6 cm wide. Wavy, wedg
shaped, saw-toothed leaves 10–30 c
long x 5–10 cm wide.

STIRLING RANGE BANKSIA
Banksia solandri

DATE	PLACE

UGUST–NOVEMBER
ERY COMMON

WATER BUSH

Bossiaea aquifolium

orest in gravel. Kalamunda to Augusta, Denmark and Williams.
hrub or tree 1–8 m high. Orange and red or yellow to brown pea flowers 10–15 mm
cross along branches. Diamond-shaped leaves 5–15 mm long x 10–20 mm wide
urrounding stem and ending in five to nine sharp points.

DATE	PLACE

JLY–NOVEMBER
OMMON

COMMON BROWN PEA

Bossiaea eriocarpa

orest and heath in sand. Shark Bay to Dunsborough, Walpole, Cape Riche and Cunderdin.
hrub 0.2–1 m high. Brown to orange-red and yellow pea flowers 10–15 mm across
ong branches. Shiny, short, narrow leaves 5–25 mm long x 1–5 mm wide curved
nder and with numerous cross-veins.

DATE	PLACE

BROAD-LEAVED BROWN PEA

Bossiaea ornata

JULY–NOVEMBER
UNCOMMON

Forest in gravel. Gingin to Augusta, Albany, Mount Barker, Kojonup and Toodyay.
Sprawling shrub 0.1–1 m high. Brown or red and yellow pea flowers 10–15 mm acros
along branches. Pointed, oval or spear-shaped leaves 2–5 cm long x 5–30 mm wide.

DATE	PLACE

LEMON-SCENTED DARWINIA

Darwinia citriodora

JUNE–JANUARY
VERY COMMON

Woodland and heath on granite outcrops. Bullsbrook to Kalamunda, Augusta, Cap
Riche and Bridgetown.
Shrub 0.2–1.5 m high. Orange to red flowers 10–20 mm long x 10 mm wid
Alternating pairs of spear-shaped, lemon-scented leaves 1–2 cm long x 2–10 mm wid

DATE	PLACE

JULY–DECEMBER
COMMON

HEART-LEAF FLAME PEA

Chorizema cordatum

Forest in clay. Jurien to Augusta, Esperance and Collie.
Shrub 0.3–1.5 m high. Orange, red or pink, and yellow pea flowers 10–15 mm across in groups along ends of branches. Wavy, oblong, prickly leaves 2–8 cm long x 5–10 mm wide.

DATE	PLACE

AUGUST–NOVEMBER
COMMON

YELLOW-EYED FLAME PEA

Chorizema dicksonii

Forest on rocky hillsides. Calingiri to Perth, Mandurah, Denmark, Albany and York.
Shrub 0.3–1 m high. Orange, red or pink and yellow pea flowers 10–15 mm across in group near ends of branches. Twisted, oval to spear-shaped leaves 5–15 mm long x 2–5 mm wide, ending in a sharp point.

DATE	PLACE

SEPTEMBER–NOVEMBER
COMMON

Forest and woodland in sand. Geraldton to Busselton and Northam.
Straggly shrub 0.5–2 m high. Orange to red and yellow pea flowers 10–15 mm across. Flat or needle-like leaf, often broad and forked at the top, 0.5–5 cm long x 2–10 mm wide.

FIRE BUSH

Daviesia physodes

DATE	PLACE

AUGUST–OCTOBER
UNCOMMON

KING-IN-HIS-CARRIAGE

Drakaea glyptodon

Woodland in sand. Jurien to Albany, Esperance and Lake Grace.
Slender plant 15–35 cm high. Single yellow-green flower 2–3 cm long and 5 mm wide with brown-purple warts and hairs on triangular lip. Heart-shaped leaf 1 cm across at base of plant.

DATE	PLACE

SEPTEMBER–OCTOBER
COMMON

Forest and heath. Busselton to Augusta.
Slender plant 25–45 cm high. Two to
eight brown, yellow and purple flowers
4–5 cm long x 2–3 cm wide. Grass-like
leaf 20–30 cm long x 5–15 mm wide at
base of plant.

DUNSBOROUGH DONKEY ORCHID

Diuris aff. *amplissima*

DATE	PLACE

AUGUST–OCTOBER
VERY COMMON

Woodland and swamps. Lancelin to
Mandurah.
Slender plant 30–60 cm high. Three to
nine brown, yellow and purple flowers
4–6 cm long x 3–5 cm wide. Grass-like
leaf 10–25 cm long x 1–2 cm wide at
base of plant.

PANSY ORCHID

Diuris magnifica

DATE	PLACE

SHOWY DRYANDRA

Dryandra formosa

MARCH–NOVEMBER
COMMON

Forest in sand or gravel. Busselton to Augusta, Cape Riche and Stirling Range.
Shrub 1–3 m high. Orange to golden flowers in a head 5–6 cm across. Soft, saw toothed leaves 10–20 cm long x 1 cm wide.

DATE	PLACE

COUCH HONEYPOT

Dryandra lindleyana

JUNE–OCTOBER
VERY COMMON

Forest, woodland and heath. Dongara to Augusta, Albany and Kulin.
Sprawling shrub 10–50 cm high. Orange to brown, yellow or pink flowers in a head 3 cm across partially hidden in leaves. Wavy, saw-toothed leaves 10–30 cm long 1–2 cm wide.

DATE	PLACE

AUGUST–NOVEMBER
COMMON

YORK ROAD POISON

Gastrolobium calycinum

orest and woodland. Mingenew to Moora, Perth, Pinjarra, Bridgetown, Cranbrook and Wyalkatchem.

hrub 0.5–2.5 m high. Orange or red and yellow pea flowers (smooth in bud) 10–15 mm cross in spike 2–4 cm long. Alternating pairs of flat or folded, oval or spear-shaped leaves –5 cm long x 5–35 mm wide, usually curled backwards and ending in a sharp point.

DATE	PLACE

AUGUST–NOVEMBER
ERY COMMON

SANDPLAIN POISON

Gastrolobium microcarpum

orest and woodland. Mingenew to Mogumber, Toodyay, Narrogin and Walpole.

hrub 0.5–2 m high. Orange or red and yellow pea flowers (silky hairy in bud) 5 mm cross in spike 3–5 cm long. Folded, spear-shaped leaves 2–4 cm long x 5–15 mm wide n groups of three along stem, usually curled backwards and ending in a sharp point.

DATE	PLACE

GOLDEN-HAIRED PEA

Jacksonia calycina

SEPTEMBER–NOVEMBER
COMMON

Woodland and heath. Stirling Range.
Shrub 0.5–1.5 m high. Orange or red and yellow pea flowers (golden hairy in bud)
10 mm across. Few thin branches 5 mm wide.

DATE	PLACE

HOLLY PEA

Jacksonia floribunda

SEPTEMBER–MAY
VERY COMMON

Woodland in sand. Northampton to Perth, Corrigin and Morawa.
Shrub 0.25–1.5 m high. Orange or brown to red and yellow pea flowers (densely
woolly white in bud) 20 mm across. Oblong, wavy, prickly, saw-toothed leaves
3–10 cm long x 1–2 cm wide.

DATE	PLACE

EPTEMBER–OCTOBER
NCOMMON

ORANGE STARS
Hibbertia stellaris

Voodland in swampy areas. Kalbarri to Perth, Augusta, Albany and Darkan.
hrub 0.2–1.5 m high. Orange or yellow flowers 10 mm across on stalks 15–20 mm
ong. Sharp, thin, wiry leaves 10–25 mm long x 1 mm wide, often hooked at end, in
lusters along stem.

DATE	PLACE

LL YEAR
ERY COMMON

Voodland and heath in sand. Wickepin
o Kojonup, Albany, Denmark, Esperance
nd Lake King.
hrub or tree 1–7 m high. Group of five
o seven orange to red or yellow tubular
owers 4 cm long x 5 mm wide at end of
ranches. Oval or spoon-shaped leaves
0–25 mm long x 5 mm wide in groups
f three around stem.

CHITTICK
Lambertia inermis

RATTLE BEAKS
Lyperanthus serratus

DATE	PLACE

SEPTEMBER–OCTOBER
VERY COMMON

Forest, woodland and heath. Perth t‹
Augusta, Albany, Esperance an‹
Katanning.
Slender plant 20–50 cm high. Three t
ten brown, green and yellow flower
25 mm long x 3–5 cm wide in a spik
5–15 cm long. Narrow leaf 20–40 cr
long x 15 mm wide at base of plant.

BACON AND EGGS
Nemcia capitata

DATE	PLACE

APRIL–OCTOBER
COMMON

Forest and woodland. Jurien to August‹
Denmark and York.
Shrub 0.2–1 m high. Orange or yello›
and red or brown pea flowers (sof
silvery hairy in bud) 10–15 mm across i
clusters. Flat or folded, spear-shaped ‹
broad, finely-veined leaves 2–10 cm lon›
x 2–15 mm wide, slightly hairy belov
and sometimes ending in a sharp point

DATE	PLACE

CTOBER–JANUARY
ERY COMMON

orest, woodland and heath in sand.
albarri to Augusta, Albany, Cape Arid
nd Corrigin.
ee 2–10 m high. Orange to gold
owers 10–15 mm long in spikes
0–25 cm long x 4 cm wide. Straight,
at leaves 5–10 cm long and 3–8 mm
ide.

CHRISTMAS TREE
Nuytsia floribunda

DATE	PLACE

UGUST–OCTOBER
NCOMMON

FLYING DUCK ORCHID
Paracaleana nigrita

orest and woodland in sand. Moora to Augusta, Albany, Esperance and Mount Barker.
lender plant 5–15 cm high. Usually one brown and green flower 15–30 mm long and
0–15 mm wide with purple warts on humped lip. Heart-shaped leaf 1 cm wide at base
f plant.

52

DATE	PLACE

LEOPARD ORCHID

Thelymitra benthamiana

SEPTEMBER–OCTOBER
UNCOMMON

Woodland near granite outcrops, creeks and swamps. Northampton to Augusta Esperance and Hyden.
Slender plant 25–40 cm high. Two to ten brown-and-yellow spotted flowers 4 cr across scattered along stem. Oval leaf 5–15 cm long x 2–3 cm wide at base of plant.

DATE	PLACE

CUSTARD ORCHID

Thelymitra villosa

SEPTEMBER–NOVEMBER
UNCOMMON

Woodland and heath. Geraldton to Augusta, Esperance and Katanning.
Slender plant 40–60 cm high. Five to twenty brown-and-yellow spotted flowers 3–4 cr across at end of stem. Hairy, oval leaf 5–10 cm long x 2–5 cm wide at base of plant.

DATE	PLACE

NE–OCTOBER
RY COMMON

PRICKLY MOSES
Acacia pulchella

rest, woodland and heath in sand and gravel. Kalbarri to Augusta, Esperance and Hyden. rub 0.5–2 m high with many brown spines 1 cm long. Numerous fluffy yellow obular flowers 5–10 mm across. Three to eight pairs of soft oblong leaflets 3–5 mm ng x 2 mm wide along leaf.

DATE	PLACE

LY–NOVEMBER
MMON

rest and woodland in sand and gravel. lbarri to Augusta, Esperance, Southern oss and Murchison.
rub or tree 2–6 m high with drooping anches. Groups of two to ten fluffy llow globular flowers 10 mm round. ng, straight, flat, green to bluish leaves –25 cm long x 5–30 mm wide with thick n in centre and often hooked at end.

ORANGE WATTLE
Acacia saligna

DATE	PLACE

COMMON CATSPAW

Anigozanthos humilis

JULY–OCTOBER
VERY COMMON

Forest and heath in sand. Kalbarri to Augusta, Hopetoun and Kulin.
Herb 0.1–1 m high. Group of five to fifteen woolly yellow and red or yellow flowe
6–10 cm long on woolly green stems 25–50 cm long. Flat, sword-shaped leaves 20–30 c
long x 1 cm wide, mostly at base of plant.

DATE	PLACE

ALBANY CATSPAW

Anigozanthos preissii

SEPTEMBER–NOVEMBER
UNCOMMON

Woodland in sand. Rocky Gully to Walpole, Albany and Mount Barker.
Herb 20–80 cm tall. Two groups of two to three woolly yellowy-green and red flowe
5 cm long on woolly brown stems 20–60 cm long. Flat, sword-shaped leaves 10–20 c
long x 2 cm wide, mostly at base of plant.

DATE	PLACE

EPTEMBER–FEBRUARY
ERY COMMON

orest, woodland and heath in sand.
hark Bay to Augusta, Bremer Bay and
Vickepin.
hrub or tree 0.5–10 m high. Yellow
owers in a cylinder 15–25 cm long x
–5 cm wide. Prickly, saw-toothed leaves
–25 cm long x 5–15 mm wide.

SLENDER BANKSIA
Banksia attenuata

DATE	PLACE

EPTEMBER–JANUARY
ERY COMMON

orest, woodland and heath in sand and
ravel. Jurien to Augusta, Cape Riche,
irling Range and Katanning.
hrub or tree 2–10 m high. Yellow
owers in a cylinder 10–40 cm long x
–10 cm wide. Saw-toothed leaves
0–45 cm long x 5–10 cm wide.

BULL BANKSIA
Banksia grandis

DATE	PLACE

HOLLY-LEAVED BANKSIA

Banksia ilicifolia

JUNE–MARCH
COMMON

Woodland in sand. Jurien to Augusta, Two Peoples Bay and Collie.
Shrub or tree 1–10 m high. Yellow and pink flowers (green and yellow in bud) turning red, in a globular head 5–9 cm across. Oval, wavy, prickly, saw-toothed or smooth leaves 3–10 cm long x 3–4 cm wide.

DATE	PLACE

JULY–DECEMBER
VERY COMMON

Forest, woodland and heath. Geraldton to Augusta, Albany, Esperance and Merredin.
Slender plant 10–30 cm high. One four yellow flowers with red marking 2–5 cm long x 2–4 cm wide. Grass-like leaf 5–15 cm long x 10–15 mm wide base of plant.

COWSLIP ORCHID

Caladenia flava

DATE	PLACE

JLY–NOVEMBER
ERY COMMON

GREY COTTONHEADS

Conostylis candicans

orest and heath in sand. Shark Bay to Augusta and Cunderdin.
lerb in tufts 50 cm high. Twenty to thirty woolly yellow flowers in globular heads
–3 cm across on woolly grey-green stems up to 50 cm long. Flat, grey, hairy, sword-
haped leaves 10–50 cm long x 2–5 mm wide, mostly at base of plant.

DATE	PLACE

UGUST–NOVEMBER
OMMON

RUSH COTTONHEADS

Conostylis juncea

'oodland in sand. Jurien to Augusta and Armadale.
erb in tufts 10-50 cm high. Five to ten bristly, woolly yellow flowers 2 cm long on
oolly stems 1–15 cm long in group at base of plant. Flat or needle-like leaves 10–50 cm
ng x 1–4 mm wide, all at base of plant.

58

DATE	PLACE

SILVERY COTTONHEADS

Conostylis pusilla

SEPTEMBER–NOVEMBER
COMMON

Forest and woodland in clay or loam. Armadale to Manjimup, Denmark, Bremer Bay, Lake Grace and Cunderdin.
Herb in tufts 5–10 cm high. Three to four woolly yellow flowers 1 cm long on woolly green stems 4 cm long. Flat, very hairy, grass-like leaves 2–4 cm long x 1 mm wide, mostly at base of plant.

DATE	PLACE

YELLOW MOUNTAIN BELL

Darwinia collina

AUGUST–FEBRUARY
COMMON

Heath on rock. Peaks at eastern end of Stirling Range.
Shrub 0.5–1.5 m high. Hanging yellow bell-shaped flowers 2–3 cm long x 2 cm wide. Crowded, oval leaves 5–10 mm long x 2–5 mm wide.

DATE	PLACE

UGUST–NOVEMBER
:OMMON

eath on hillsides. Rocky Gully to
)enmark, Hopetoun and Kojonup.
hrub 0.3–1 m high. Five to ten yellow
nd red to orange pea flowers 10 mm
cross surrounded by 3 leaf-like cups at
nd of branches. Wedge-shaped leaves
–10 cm long x 1–2 cm wide in rings of
hree around stem.

RATTLE PEA
Daviesia oppositifolia

DATE	PLACE

UGUST–OCTOBER
ERY COMMON

COMMON DONKEY ORCHID
Diuris corymbosa

orest, woodland and swamps. Dongara to Augusta, Albany and Esperance.
ender plant 30–45 cm high. Two to eight yellow and red to orange flowers 2–3 cm
ng x 2 cm wide. Grass-like leaf 10–20 cm long x 5–10 mm wide at base of plant.

DATE	PLACE

JULY–JANUARY
COMMON

Heath in sand or clay. Stirling Range t
Albany, Cape Le Grand and Ongerup.
Shrub 0.5–2 m high. Bright yellow t
orange flowers in a head 5 cm acros:
Wavy, irregular, deeply-toothed, prickl
wedge-shaped leaves 5–10 cm long
2–3 cm wide.

PRICKLY DRYANDRA
Dryandra falcata

DATE	PLACE

AUGUST–DECEMBER
COMMON

Woodland in sand. Arthur River t
Augusta and Esperance.
Shrub 0.5–2 m high. Crowded yellow (
orange and red pea flowers 10 m|
across at end of branches. Straight leav(
5–10 mm long x 1–2 mm wide crowde
around stem.

BEAUTIFUL YELLOW PEA
Eutaxia densifolia

DATE	PLACE

JLY–NOVEMBER
NCOMMON

GOLDEN GUINEA FLOWER

Hibbertia aurea

orest and woodland in gravel or rock. Northampton to Busselton, Nannup and everley.

hrub 0.5–1 m high. Yellow flowers 15–20 mm across. Few straight leaves 10–20 mm ong x 1–2 mm wide, curled over lengthwise and ending in a sharp point.

DATE	PLACE

JNE–MARCH
ERY COMMON

CUTLEAF HIBBERTIA

Hibbertia cuneiformis

orest, woodland and heath. Perth to Augusta, Esperance and Manjimup.

hrub 1–3 m high. Yellow flowers 25–40 mm across. Triangular to wedge-shaped leaves 0–30 mm long x 5–10 mm wide, often with several teeth near the top.

DATE	PLACE

LONG-LEAVED GUINEA FLOWER

Hibbertia huegelii

MARCH–DECEMBER
VERY COMMON

Forest, woodland and heath. Morawa to Mingenew, Eneabba, Bunbury, Rocky Gully and Brookton.
Sprawling shrub 10–60 cm high. Yellow flowers 20–35 mm across. Straight, flat pointed leaves 2–6 cm long x 1–2 mm wide, curled over lengthwise and sometimes ending in a sharp point.

DATE	PLACE

YELLOW BUTTERCUP

Hibbertia hypericoides

APRIL–DECEMBER
VERY COMMON

Forest, woodland and heath. Kalbarri to Augusta, Mount Barker, Bremer Bay, Arthur River and Paynes Find.
Shrub 0.2–1 m high. Yellow flowers 15–25 mm across. Straight leaves 5–15 mm long x 1–4 mm wide, curled over lengthwise, smooth on top and rough or hairy below.

DATE	PLACE

MAY–FEBRUARY
VERY COMMON

HAIRY YELLOW PEA

Gompholobium tomentosum

Forest, woodland and heath in sand. Shark Bay to Augusta, Hopetoun and Corrigin. Shrub 0.3–1 m high. Hairy yellow pea flowers 10 mm across at end of branches. Hairy or smooth leaves with 5–9 straight leaflets 5–20 mm long x 0.5 mm wide, ending in a sharp point.

DATE	PLACE

SEPTEMBER–DECEMBER
UNCOMMON

Forest and heath in sand or gravel. Bullsbrook to Augusta, Cape Arid, Gnowangerup and Toodyay. Shrub 0.2–2 m high. Yellow flowers in globular heads 2–3 cm across, set amongst leaves at top of stem. Thick spoon-shaped leaves 10–20 cm long x 1–2 cm wide.

SPOON-LEAVED CONEFLOWER

Isopogon attenuatus

DATE	PLACE

GRANNY'S BONNET

Isotropis cuneifolia

JULY–NOVEMBER
COMMON

Woodland and heath in sand or gravel. Shark Bay to Augusta, Cape Le Grand and Wickepin.

Slender plant 5–30 cm high. Single yellow to orange and red pea flower 15–25 mm across, with red lines on back, at end of stalk 5–10 cm long. Irregular, straight or spoon-shaped leaves 1–5 cm long x 1–25 mm wide divided into lobes, mostly at base of plant.

DATE	PLACE

STINKWOOD

Jacksonia sternbergiana

ALL YEAR
COMMON

Forest, woodland and heath in sand. Northampton to Harvey, Boyup Brook, Kojonup and Kulin.

Spindly shrub 1.5–5 m high with hanging branches. Orange-yellow pea flowers 10 mm across. Sharp, pointed, needle-like, blue-green leaf-like branches 2–4 cm long x 1 mm wide.

DATE	PLACE

EPTEMBER–OCTOBER
JNCOMMON

YELLOW MOUNTAIN PEA

Nemcia crenulata

leath in rocky soil. Denmark to Stirling Range and Hopetoun.
hrub 1–2.5 m high. Yellow and red pea flowers (silvery hairy in bud) 20 mm across in
lusters along branches. Oval leaves 3–5 cm long x 2–3 cm wide, in groups of 3 or 4
long stem and ending in a small point.

DATE	PLACE

UGUST–SEPTEMBER
ERY COMMON

Voodland and heath. Darkan to Stirling
ange.
hrub 0.5–2 m high. Yellow and red or
range pea flowers (silky silver in bud)
0–15 mm across in clusters. Slightly
lded, broad leaves 15–25 mm long x
–10 mm wide, in groups of 3 along
em and ending in a small point.

BUSHY YELLOW PEA

Nemcia pulchella

DATE	PLACE

VEINED YELLOW PEA

Nemcia reticulata

MAY–NOVEMBER
COMMON

Woodland and heath in sand. Kalbarri to Mandurah and York.
Shrub 0.2–1 m high. Yellow or orange and red or brown pea flowers (coarsely silver hairy in bud) 10–15 mm across in clusters. Flat or folded, spear-shaped or oval coarsely-veined leaves 1–5 cm long x 5–20 mm wide, opposite each other or in groups of 3 or 4 along stem, sometimes ending in a sharp point.

DATE	PLACE

SILKY YELLOW PEA

Nemcia retusa

AUGUST–NOVEMBER
COMMON

Woodland and heath. Bindoon to Mount Barker, Stirling Range and Toodyay.
Shrub 1–2 m high. Yellow and red to orange pea flowers (woolly white or gold in bud) 10–15 mm across in clusters at end of branches. Folded, wedge-shaped or broad, straight, leaves 1–3 cm long x 5–10 mm wide, ending in a slight depression or notch

DATE	PLACE

LL YEAR
COMMON

orest, woodland and heath in sand and
ravel. Dongara to Augusta, Cape Arid
nd Kulin.
lant 30–80 cm high. Yellow flowers 1
m long in triangular spikes 1–3 cm
cross at the end of three-sided stems
0–60 cm long. Straight, channelled
eaves 20–60 cm long and 2–3 mm wide,
ll at base of plant.

SEMAPHORE SEDGE

Mesomelaena tetragona

DATE	PLACE

UGUST–JANUARY
COMMON

FERN HEATH

Oligarrhena micrantha

eath in sand. Frankland to Albany, Cape Arid and Ravensthorpe.
hrub 10–60 cm high. Crowded yellow to white tubular flowers 1–2 mm long in spikes
–20 cm long at end of branches. Scale-like leaves 1–2 mm long x 0.5 mm wide closely
ressed against stem.

DATE	PLACE

YELLOW FLAG

Patersonia umbrosa var. *xanthina*

AUGUST–DECEMBER
COMMON

Forest in sand or gravel. Perth to Augusta, Walpole and Collie.
Plant 30–90 cm high. Yellow flowers 5–7 cm across in a green head 5–10 cm long on
a stalk 30–80 cm long. Flat, grass-like leaves 30–90 cm long x 5 mm wide, all at base
of plant. Variety *umbrosa* is purple.

DATE	PLACE

PLUME PETROPHILE

Petrophile serruriae

JULY–DECEMBER
COMMON

Forest, woodland and heath. Geraldton to Augusta, Cape Riche, Stirling Range and York.
Shrub 0.2–1.5 m high. Yellow to white or pink flowers 1–2 cm long in spike 5–20 cm
long x 4–6 cm across. Prickly leaves 1–3 cm long divided into many sharp, pointed
needle-like sections 5 mm long x 1 mm wide.

DATE	PLACE

JLY–JANUARY
COMMON

Woodland and heath. York to Perth, Augusta, Cape Arid and Hyden.
Shrub 0.5–3 m high. Several fluffy yellow to white flowers in oval heads 2 cm long 2 cm wide along branch. Prickly leaves –5 cm long, divided into three to nine lobes 5–10 mm long x 5 mm wide and ending in a sharp point.

SCALY PETROPHILE
Petrophile squamata

DATE	PLACE

AUGUST–NOVEMBER
COMMON

Forest, woodland and heath in gravel or clay. Eneabba to Augusta, Wagin and Moora.
Shrub 0.2–1 m high. Several sticky, hairy yellow to white flowers in oval heads 2 cm long x 1.5 cm wide. Flat leaves 3–6 cm long divided into eight to fifteen segments 5–10 mm long x 2–3 mm wide and ending in a sharp point.

STICKY PETROPHILE
Petrophile striata

DATE	PLACE

SCENTED BANJINE

Pimelea suaveolens

JULY–NOVEMBER
UNCOMMON

Forest and woodland in sand or gravel. Jurien to Augusta, Albany, Salmon Gums and Coolgardie.
Shrub 0.2–1.5 m high. Hanging yellow to green flowers in globular heads 2–5 cm across. Flat, spear-shaped leaves 0.5–3 cm long x 2–5 mm wide.

DATE	PLACE

STRIPED BUSH PEA

Pultenaea strobilifera

SEPTEMBER–OCTOBER
UNCOMMON

Woodland and heath in sand. Busselton to Denmark, Cape Arid and Lake Grace.
Shrub 10–50 cm high. Yellow and red to orange or brown pea flowers (hairy brown bud) 10–15 mm across in globular head at top of branches. Blunt, straight, needle-like leaves 5–10 mm long x 1 mm wide.

DATE	PLACE

.UGUST–DECEMBER
ERY COMMON

COMMON BUTTERCUP

Ranunculus colonorum

wampy areas. Yanchep to Augusta, Albany, Mount Barker and Collie.
lender plant 20–80 cm high. Glossy, shiny yellow flowers 2–3 cm across at end of stalk
–20 cm long. Long leaves, divided into lobes, 3–8 cm long x 2–5 mm wide.

DATE	PLACE

JNE–SEPTEMBER
OMMON

/oodland and heath in sand or gravel.
ullsbrook to Perth, Armadale and
Jundaring.
hrub 0.3–1 m high. Yellow tubular
owers 3 mm long in a 1–3 cm long
ike above leaves at the end of a stalk
5–70 cm long. Prickly, wavy, wedge-
aped leaves 10–30 cm long at base of
ant, divided into three to nine lobes
-3 cm long x 2–5 mm wide.

GRANITE SYNAPHEA

Synaphea acutiloba

DATE	PLACE

COMMON VELLEIA

Velleia trinervis

JULY–FEBRUARY
VERY COMMON

Forest and woodland in damp soils. Mingenew to Augusta, Cape Arid and Kellerberrir
Plant 10–50 cm high. Yellow to orange and brown flowers 10–15 mm across on rec
brown stems 5–40 cm long. Smooth to fuzzy, straight or spoon-shaped leaves 5–20 cr
long x 5–25 mm wide, all at base of plant.

DATE	PLACE

BRISTLY YELLOW FEATHERFLOWER

Verticordia acerosa

AUGUST–NOVEMBER
COMMON

Forest and heath. Coorow to Lancelin, Bunbury, Bremer Bay, Esperance and Southern Cros
Shrub 0.2–1 m high. Round yellow flowers (turning orange to red-brown with ag
5–10 mm across with feather-like petals in umbrella-shaped head at end of branche
Blunt, needle-like or broad leaves 5–15 mm long x 0.5–2 mm wide.

DATE	PLACE

OCTOBER–FEBRUARY
COMMON

FLANNEL FLOWER

Actinotus leucocephalus

Forest, woodland and heath in sand and gravel. Billabong to Dongara, Waroona and Paynes Find, and Cranbrook to Albany and Ongerup.
Plant 10–50 cm high. Woolly white flowers 2–5 cm across. Slightly hairy leaves 2–5 cm long divided into straight segments 1–3 cm long x 1–2 mm wide.

DATE	PLACE

MAY–DECEMBER
VERY COMMON

PEPPERMINT

Agonis flexuosa

Forest and woodland in sand. Perth to Augusta, Bremer Bay and Rocky Gully.
Tree or shrub 1–15 m high. Groups of two to five white flowers 5–10 mm across near ends of branches. Flat, spear-shaped leaves 2–10 cm long x 5–10 mm wide.

DATE	PLACE

GIANT ANDERSONIA

Andersonia axilliflora

SEPTEMBER–NOVEMBER
VERY COMMON

Heath on rock. Peaks at eastern end of Stirling Range.
Shrub 0.5–2 m high. White flowers 10 mm long hidden within white leaves at the end of branches. Crowded, sword-shaped leaves 3–6 cm long x 1–2 cm wide, ending in sharp point.

DATE	PLACE

SPINY ANDERSONIA

Andersonia echinocephala

SEPTEMBER–NOVEMBER
VERY COMMON

Heath on rock. Stirling Range to Hopetoun.
Shrub 0.3–1.5 m high. White flowers 10 mm long hidden within white leaves at the end of branches. Prickly, twisted leaves 2–3 cm long x 5 mm wide, ending in a sharp point.

DATE	PLACE

ALL YEAR
COMMON

STICKY TAILFLOWER

Anthocercis viscosa

Woodland and heath on granite outcrops near the coast. Walpole to Cape Arid.
Shrub 0.5–4 m high. Tubular white flowers 3–4 cm across. Sticky broad or spear-shaped
leaves 2–5 cm long x 1–3 cm wide.

DATE	PLACE

ALL YEAR
COMMON

KICK BUSH

Astroloma pallidum

Woodland. Jurien to Augusta, Cape Riche, Jerramungup and Hyden.
Low straggly or upright shrub 2–30 cm high. Tubular white, pink or red flowers with
woolly tips 10–15 mm long. Flat, toothed, spear-shaped leaves 1–2 cm long x 2–4 mm
wide, ending in a sharp point.

DATE	PLACE

MAY–FEBRUARY
COMMON

CAMPHOR MYRTLE

Baeckea camphorosmae

Woodland and heath in sand or gravel Mingenew to Donnybrook, Albany and Wongan Hills.
Shrub 0.2–1.2 cm tall. White or pink flowers 10 mm across in spike 10 cm long at end of branches. Crowded, straight, three-sided leaves 2–7 mm long x 1 mm wide, all on side branches.

DATE	PLACE

AUGUST–NOVEMBER
VERY COMMON

PINCUSHIONS

Borya sphaerocephala

Heath in sand or clay or on granite outcrops. Kalbarri to Bunbury, Windy Harbour, Lake King, Southern Cross and Paynes Find.
Herb 5–30 cm high in clumps or extensive mat. Many white flowers in globular head 10–15 mm across at end of stalk 10–25 cm long. Straight, un-pinched, needle-like leaves 5–15 cm long x 1 mm wide, near top of stem and ending in a sharp point.

DATE	PLACE

ULY–NOVEMBER
VERY COMMON

MILKMAIDS

Burchardia umbellata

orest and woodland. Geraldton to Augusta, Albany, Mount Barker, Collie and Wongan Hills. Herb 10–70 cm high. Two to six white flowers 3 cm across at the end of stalks 10–25 mm ong in a head 5–7 cm across at end of a stem 30–70 cm long. Straight, channelled eaves 15–30 cm long x 3–5 mm wide, all at base of plant.

DATE	PLACE

EPTEMBER–NOVEMBER
ERY COMMON

orest and woodland. Gingin to Busselton, Jannup, Stirling Range and Wagin. Iender plant 35–60 cm high. One to our white flowers 10–15 cm long x –10 cm wide with red markings and ong fringes on lip. Grass-like leaf 20–25 cm ong x 5–15 mm wide at base of plant. Ine of many very similar orchids in aladenia longicauda group.

WHITE SPIDER ORCHID

Caladenia longicauda subsp. *longicauda*

DATE	PLACE

JULY–NOVEMBER
COMMON

WHITE STARFLOWER
Calytrix tetragona

Woodland in sand. Collie to Augusta
Albany, Caiguna, Kalgoorlie and
Southern Cross.
Shrub 0.2–1.5 m high. Masses of white
star flowers with pink tinge 10–15 mm
across at end of branch. Straight, smooth
or hairy leaves 3–6 mm long x 1 mm
wide, ending in a sharp point.

DATE	PLACE

AUGUST–DECEMBER
COMMON

MANY-FLOWERED SMOKEBUSH
Conospermum floribundum

Woodland and heath in sand or gravel
Boyup Brook to Albany, Hopetoun and
Lake Grace.
Shrub 0.2–1 m high. Woolly white
flowers with blue or pinkish tinge
forming feather-duster-shaped head
5–8 cm across. Blunt, incurved needle-
like leaves 10–15 mm long x 1mm wide

DATE	PLACE

MARCH–SEPTEMBER
VERY COMMON

Forest, woodland and heath in sand or
gravel. Eneabba to Busselton, Nannup
and Wongan Hills.
Shrub 20–70 cm high. Hanging red- or
purple-tipped white cone-shaped flowers
10–15 mm long x 3 mm wide. Spear-
shaped leaves 20–35 mm long x 5 mm
wide, ending in a sharp point.

PEARL FLOWER

Conostephium pendulum

DATE	PLACE

AUGUST–NOVEMBER
COMMON

WHITE COTTONHEADS

Conostylis setosa

Forest in gravel. Bindoon to Perth, Mount Barker and Katanning.
Plant in tufts 10–40 cm high. Ten to fifteen woolly white to red or purplish-cream tubular
flowers 15–20 mm long in head 4–6 cm across on woolly grey stems 25–40 cm long.
Flat, spiny, sword-shaped leaves 10–30 cm long x 2–4 mm wide, mostly at base of plant.

DATE	PLACE

POM-POM DARWINIA
Darwinia vestita

MAY–DECEMBER
VERY COMMON

Woodland and heath in sand or gravel. Beverley to Bunbury, Augusta, Cape Arid and Narrogin.
Shrub 0.2–1 m high. White to pink or red flowers in globular heads 1–2 cm across. Thick, crowded, three-sided leaves 2–4 mm long x 0.5 mm wide.

DATE	PLACE

PINEAPPLE BUSH
Dasypogon bromeliifolius

JULY–JANUARY
VERY COMMON

Forest, woodland and heath in sand or gravel. Jurien to Augusta, Hopetoun, Collie and Armadale.
Plant 0.3–1 m high in tufted clumps. Many white to cream flowers (hairy brown to black in bud) in globular head 3–5 cm across at end of stalk 30–55 cm long. Straight, flat, spiny leaves 10–40 cm long x 5–10 mm wide, ending in a sharp point.

DATE	PLACE

ULY–SEPTEMBER
COMMON

orest, woodland and heath in sand.
neabba to Collie, Armadale and Three
prings.
Herb 10–50 cm high. White flowers
0–15 mm across at end of stalk 5 cm
ong. Sticky, hairy, oval or fan-shaped
eaves 5–10 mm across on stalk
–30 mm long.

LEAFY SUNDEW

Drosera stolonifera subsp. *porrecta*

DATE	PLACE

UGUST–DECEMBER
COMMON

BLUE DEVILS

Eryngium pinnatifidum

Woodland and heath. Northampton to Augusta, Albany and Kellerberrin.
Shrub 20–50 cm high. White to blue or purple flowers in globular heads 1–3 cm across
n a stalk 15–30 cm long, surrounded by sharp pointed floral leaves 1–3 cm long. Flat
eaves 5–25 cm long, divided into lobes 1–3 cm long x 1–2 mm wide, each ending in
sharp point.

82

DATE	PLACE

AUGUST–DECEMBER
VERY COMMON

JARRAH
Eucalyptus marginata

Forest and woodland. Jurien to Augusta, Bremer Bay, Kojonup and Kulin.
Tree 2–45 m high. White flowers 1–2 cm across with brown cap before flowering.
Curved, spear-shaped leaves 5–10 cm long x 1–3 cm wide with thick margin and vein
1 mm from edge.

DATE	PLACE

AUGUST–OCTOBER
VERY COMMON

Woodland and heath. Busselton to Cape
Riche, Ongerup and Narrogin.
Shrub 1–2 m high. White to cream
flowers in clusters 10–15 mm across.
Thick, spear-shaped leaves 4–8 cm long
x 5–10 mm wide with 3 veins. Hard
oval, woody nut 2 cm long x 1 cm wide
with long beak at end.

WHITE-VEINED HAKEA
Hakea ambigua

DATE	PLACE

JLY–NOVEMBER
'ERY COMMON

Voodland and heath in sand or on
ranite rocks. Moora to Perth and
Vongan Hills.
hrub 0.5–3 m high. White flowers with
ink tinge 1–2 cm long x 1 cm wide
long leafless branch 1–3 m long.
traight, pointed silky leaves 5–15 cm
ong x 1–5 mm wide.

SPINDLY GREVILLEA

Grevillea endlicheriana

DATE	PLACE

JNE–NOVEMBER
OMMON

Voodland and heath in gravel in rocky
reas. Jurien to Bunbury, Albany,
erramungup and Kellerberrin.
hrub 0.2–1 m high. Woolly white
owers 1–2 cm long x 1 cm wide.
traight, folded, hairy leaves 0.5–5 cm
ong x 1–10 mm wide, usually ending in
sharp point.

WOOLLY-FLOWERED GREVILLEA

Grevillea pilulifera

DATE	PLACE

MAY–OCTOBER
COMMON

CATKIN GREVILLEA

Grevillea synapheae

Woodland and heath. Eneabba to Perth, Jarrahdale, Toodyay and Three Springs.
Sprawling to erect shrub 0.2–1 m high. Many creamy white to yellow flowers in
cylinder 1–6 cm long x 1–2 cm wide. Wedge-shaped leaves 5–20 cm long x 1–6 cm
wide divided into three straight or wedge-shaped lobes 1–3 cm long x 5–10 mm wide
each ending in a sharp point.

DATE	PLACE

AUGUST–OCTOBER
UNCOMMON

Forest and woodland in sand or gravel.
Perth to Darkan, Wagin and York.
Shrub 0.5–1.5 m high. Hanging whit
flowers with pinkish-violet ting
1.5–3 cm long x 1–2 cm wide. Prickl
leaves 2–6 cm long x 1–6 cm wid
divided into two to seven triangula
lobes 5–10 mm long x 3–5 mm wide
each ending in a sharp point.

TASSEL GREVILLEA

Grevillea tenuiflora

DATE	PLACE

JLY–DECEMBER
OMMON

MAYWEED SUNRAY

Hyalosperma cotula

orest, woodland and heath. Kalbarri to Augusta, Albany and Yalgoo.
Iender plant 5–30 cm tall. Round white, yellow or pinkish flowers with yellow centres
–3 cm across at end of stalk. Wiry, straight leaves 5–20 mm long x 1 mm wide along
:em.

DATE	PLACE

JNE–NOVEMBER
OMMON

orest, woodland, heath and creek beds.
orthampton to Augusta, Bremer Bay
nd Wongan Hills.
nrub 0.2–1.5 m high. White to pink
owers 5–10 mm across in spikes
)–30 cm long along stem. Pointed,
Ided, needle-like leaves 15–35 mm
ng x 1–2 mm wide.

WHITE MYRTLE

Hypocalymma angustifolium

DATE	PLACE

SEPTEMBER–JANUARY
COMMON

Forest, woodland and heath. Kalbarri t
Augusta, Esperance and Southern Cross
Slender plant 10–60 cm high. White
pink or blue flowers 2–3 cm across i
spike 5–10 cm long. Thin, straight leave
5–25 mm long x 1 mm wide.

WOODBRIDGE POISON
Isotoma hypocrateriformis

DATE	PLACE

SEPTEMBER–OCTOBER
VERY COMMON

Forest and swampy areas. Kalbarri t
Augusta, Albany, Esperance an
Merredin.
Slender plant 10–30 cm high. One
two white flowers with red ears 1–2 c
long x 1 cm wide. Shiny, oval le
6–10 cm long x 3 cm wide at base
plant.

RABBIT ORCHID
Leptoceras menziesii

DATE	PLACE

APRIL–OCTOBER
COMMON

orest and woodland in sand on granite
ocks. Perth to Bridgetown, Albany,
Narrogin and Mundaring.
hrub 10–70 cm tall. White to pink
ubular flowers 5–10 mm long x 2–4 mm
vide with woolly tips in clusters at end of
branch. Toothed, flat, spear-shaped
eaves 5–10 mm long and 2–3 mm wide,
nding in a sharp point.

PEARLY BEARD-HEATH

Leucopogon strictus

DATE	PLACE

MAY–NOVEMBER
UNCOMMON

Woodland. Gingin to Perth, Augusta,
Cape Arid, Boyup Brook and Northam.
Herb 25–70 cm high. White, scented
ubular flowers 5–10 mm long in closely-
paced rings around stem in spike 5–15 cm
ong on stalk 10–60 cm long. Straight
eaves 20–65 cm long x 1–3 mm wide,
ll at base of plant.

DARK MAT RUSH

Lomandra nigricans

DATE	PLACE

WHITE BANJINE

Pimelea ciliata

AUGUST–NOVEMBER
COMMON

Forest, woodland and heath in gravel or clay. Bindoon to Armadale, Augusta, Albany
Narrogin and Wongan Hills.
Shrub 0.3–1 m high. White or pale pink (rare) flowers in erect globular heads 2–3 cr
across. Flat, spear-shaped leaves 1–2 cm long x 2–7 mm wide, bent at the tip.

DATE	PLACE

MOUNTAIN BANJINE

Pimelea lehmanniana

AUGUST–DECEMBER
UNCOMMON

Forest, woodland and heath. Kalamunda to Busselton, Walpole, Hopetoun, Kojonu
and Darkan.
Shrub 0.2–1 m high. Erect or hanging hairy white to pale yellow or pinkish flowers i
globular heads 4–6 cm across. Flat, spear-shaped leaves 10–35 mm long x 2–10 mr
wide, ending in a sharp point.

DATE	PLACE

JULY–DECEMBER
COMMON

REED TRIGGERPLANT

Stylidium junceum

Woodland and heath in sand and clay. Dongara to Augusta, Cape Riche, Stirling Range, Rocky Gully and New Norcia.
Plant 0.1–1 m high. White to cream or pink flowers 5–15 mm long x 10–15 mm wide in a conical or cylindrical head 1–4 cm long x 4 cm wide at end of stalk 0.1–1 m long. Straight, pointed leaves 5–40 mm long x 1–2 mm wide in a ring around stem at base of plant.

DATE	PLACE

AUGUST–DECEMBER
UNCOMMON

COW KICKS

Stylidium schoenoides

Forest, woodland and heath in sand or gravel. Eneabba to Augusta, Cape Le Grand and Kulin. Slender plant 10–40 cm high. White to yellow flowers 15–40 mm long and 10–15 mm wide at end of hairy stalk 10–35 cm long. Grass-like leaves 10–30 cm long x 2–3 mm wide in a ring around stem at base of plant.

DATE	PLACE

HIDDEN FEATHERFLOWER

Verticordia habrantha

AUGUST–DECEMBER
VERY COMMON

Heath in sand or clay. Harvey to Busselton, Walpole, Munglinup and Hyden.
Shrub 20–70 cm high. White flowers (sometimes with pink tinge) 5–10 mm across with
numerous hairs below petals. Warty, thick, straight to oval, three-sided leaves 2–10 mm
long x 1–2 mm wide.

DATE	PLACE

SOUTHERN CROSS

Xanthosia rotundifolia

JUNE–MARCH
COMMON

Woodland and heath in gravel or rock. Walpole to Albany and Stirling Range.
Shrub 20–90 cm high. Group of five white flower heads 15 mm across forming a cross
3–5 cm across. Toothed, circular or oval leaves 2–6 cm long x 1–4 cm wide.

DATE	PLACE

JULY–FEBRUARY
VERY COMMON

Forest and heath in sand or gravel. Kalbarri to Perth, Arthur River, Katanning, Lake Grace and Quairading. Shrub 2–4 m high. Greeny-yellow to pink flowers with red tips 2–3 cm long. Leaves 1–3 cm long divided into five to seven soft, hairy, needle-like leaflets 10 mm long x 1 mm wide, sometimes ending in swollen yellow or red tips.

COMMON WOOLLYBUSH

Adenanthos cygnorum

DATE	PLACE

SEPTEMBER–NOVEMBER
VERY COMMON

Forest and woodland. Jurien to Augusta, Walpole and York, and Rocky Gully to Mount Barker and Cape Arid. Palm-like plant 0.5–3.5 m high with trunk up to 3 m high. Cylindrical or oval green cone 30–50 cm long x 15–25 cm wide in the centre of the plant. Palm-like leaves 1–2 m long x 10–30 cm wide at top of trunk.

ZAMIA

Macrozamia riedlei

BIRD ORCHID
Pterostylis barbata

DATE	PLACE

JULY–OCTOBER
UNCOMMON

Forest. Bindoon to Augusta, Albany and Manjimup.
Slender plant 20–30 cm high. Green flower 4–5 cm long and 2–3 cm wide with only a few hairs on protruding tongue. Spear-shaped leaves 2–3 cm long x 1 cm wide.

JUG ORCHID
Pterostylis recurva

DATE	PLACE

AUGUST–OCTOBER
COMMON

Forest and woodland. Geraldton to Augusta, Esperance and Merredin.
Slender plant 30–60 cm high. One to four green or reddish-brown and white flowers 3 cm long and 3 cm wide. Spear-shaped leaves 1–5 cm long x 1 cm wide.

DATE	PLACE

JUNE–NOVEMBER
COMMON

POSY STARFLOWER
Calytrix leschenaultii

Woodland and heath in sand or gravel. Kalbarri to Busselton, Denmark, Cape Arid, Southern Cross and Paynes Find.
Shrub 0.2–1 m high. Masses of purple or blue to pink star flowers with yellow or red centres 10–15 mm across and red tails. Spear-shaped to straight, three-sided leaves 1–4 mm long x 1 mm wide.

DATE	PLACE

JULY–OCTOBER
VERY COMMON

BLUE SQUILL
Chamaescilla corymbosa

Forest, woodland and heath in moist sand and on rock. Kalbarri to Augusta, Esperance and Corrigin.
Herb 5–40 cm high. Blue flowers 15–20 mm across in umbrella-like head on a stalk 5–30 cm long. Four to seven flat, oblong leaves 5–10 cm long x 2–10 mm wide, all at base of plant.

DATE	PLACE

AUGUST–DECEMBER
COMMON

Heath in sand, gravel or rock. Albany t
Stirling Range.
Shrub 0.2–1 m high. Slightly hairy dee
blue flowers 3–5 mm long clustered a
the top of branches in bunches 5–10 cr
long x 3–5 cm wide. Blunt needle-lik
leaves 1–2 cm long x 1–2 mm wide.

STIRLING RANGE SMOKEBUSH

Conospermum coerulescens subsp. *dorrienii*

DATE	PLACE

SEPTEMBER–NOVEMBER
UNCOMMON

BLUE-TIPPED SMOKEBUSH

Conospermum spectabile

Woodland and heath in sand. Stirling Range.
Shrub 0.5–1 m high. Woolly white flowers with blue or purple tips 5–10 mm long i
spikes 5–10 cm long x 3–5 cm across at the end of branches. Incurved needle-lik
leaves 10–15 mm long x 1 mm wide.

DATE	PLACE

AUGUST–OCTOBER
COMMON

Swamps and granite outcrops. Mogumber to Perth, Collie and Armadale. Shrub 0.2–1 m high. Pale blue to white flowers in spikes 1–4 cm long x 1–2 cm across at the end of leafless stems 0.5–1 m long. Thin, reed-like leaves 10–20 cm long x 1 mm wide, all at base of plant.

SLENDER SMOKEBUSH
Conospermum huegelii

DATE	PLACE

OCTOBER–DECEMBER
COMMON

Forest, woodland and heath. Exmouth to Augusta, Eucla, Wiluna and Mingenew. Herb 0.3–1.5 m high. Hanging blue to purple flowers 5–20 mm long x 5–10 mm wide on branched leafless stalk up to 1 m long. Flat, sword-shaped leaves 50–85 cm long x 10–15 mm wide. Blue berry-like fruit 10 mm long x 5 mm wide.

BLUEBERRY LILY
Dianella revoluta

DATE	PLACE

BLUE CHINA ORCHID

Cyanicula gemmata

SEPTEMBER–OCTOBER
VERY COMMON

Forest, woodland and heath. Kalbarri to Augusta, Esperance and Kulin.
Slender plant 5–15 cm high. One to three blue flowers 2–5 cm across. Hairy oval leaf (purple underneath) 2–4 cm long x 1–2 cm wide at base of plant.

DATE	PLACE

AUGUST–OCTOBER
UNCOMMON

Forest, woodland and granite outcrops. Perth to Augusta, Esperance and Katanning.
Slender plant 15–40 cm high. One to four blue flowers 3–5 cm across. Silky spear-shaped leaf 5–10 cm long x 2 cm wide at base of plant.

SILKY BLUE ORCHID

Cyanicula sericea

DATE	PLACE

JLY–NOVEMBER
COMMON

WINGED-STEM DAMPIERA
Dampiera alata

orest and woodland in sand or clay. Cataby to Perth, Augusta, Bremer Bay, nowangerup and New Norcia.
hrub 10–60 cm high with two-winged stems. Blue to purple flowers 10–15 mm cross, woolly grey in bud. Smooth or toothed, straight or spear-shaped leaves 1–5 cm ong x 5–20 mm wide.

DATE	PLACE

1AY–DECEMBER
COMMON

COMMON DAMPIERA
Dampiera linearis

orest and woodland in sand or clay. Northampton to Augusta, Two Peoples Bay, avensthorpe and Southern Cross.
nrub 10–60 cm high. Blue to purple flowers 10–20 mm across, woolly grey in bud. Smooth r toothed, straight, wedge-shaped or spear-shaped leaves 1–4 cm long x 2–15 mm wide.

DATE	PLACE

KARRI DAMPIERA

Dampiera hederacea

JUNE–FEBRUARY
UNCOMMON

Forest in wet areas. Waroona to Augusta, Bremer Bay, Mount Barker and Collie. Prostrate to erect shrub 0.2–1 m high. Blue to purple flowers 10–15 mm across, wooll brown in bud. Toothed, oval to triangular leaves 1–3 cm long x 1–3 cm wide, rough c smooth above and woolly grey-white below.

DATE	PLACE

ANGLED-STEM DAMPIERA

Dampiera trigona

AUGUST–JANUARY
COMMON

Heath in sand or clay. Mogumber to Augusta, Albany, Rocky Gully and Collie. Upright or sprawling shrub 5–50 cm high with three-sided stems. Blue to purple flowe 10–15 mm across, hairy grey in bud. Straight or spear-shaped leaves 1–5 cm long 2–5 mm wide.

DATE	PLACE

AUGUST–OCTOBER
VERY COMMON

Forest, woodland and heath. Kalbarri to Albany, Esperance and Merredin.
Slender plant 15–30 cm high. One to three glossy purple flowers 2–3 cm across (spotted on back). Grass-like leaf 4–8 cm long x 1 cm wide at base of plant.

PURPLE ENAMEL ORCHID
Elythranthera brunonis

DATE	PLACE

JUNE–OCTOBER
COMMON

Forest and woodland in sand. Eneabba to Augusta, Two Peoples Bay and Pemberton.
Twining vine. Blue to purple pea flowers with yellow-green "eye" 10 mm across in a hanging spike 5–20 cm long. Shiny, pear-shaped leaves 3–10 cm long x 1.5–5 cm wide in groups of 3–5 along stem and ending in a point.

NATIVE WISTERIA
Hardenbergia comptoniana

DATE	PLACE

JUNE–OCTOBER
UNCOMMON

Forest, woodland and heath in sand o
gravel on hillsides. Toodyay to Perth
Augusta, Albany and York.
Shrub 10–60 cm high. Blue to purple pe
flowers 10 mm across in clusters alon
branch. Oval, wavy, prickly, toothe
leaves 2–8 cm long x 1–4 cm wide.

HOLLY-LEAVED HOVEA
Hovea chorizemifolia

DATE	PLACE

AUGUST–DECEMBER
COMMON

TREE HOVEA
Hovea elliptica

Forest and woodland. Harvey to Busselton, Augusta, Bremer Bay, Mount Barker an
Nannup.
Shrub or tree 0.5–3 m high. Blue to purple pea flowers 10 mm across in clusters alon
branch. Oval leaves 5–10 cm long x 1–4 cm wide.

DATE	PLACE

MAY–OCTOBER
COMMON

Forest, woodland and heath. Geraldton to Augusta, Rocky Gully, Bremer Bay, Cape Arid, Wagin and Northam.
Shrub 0.2–2 m high. Blue to purple pea flowers 10 mm across in spike 5–30 cm long at end of branch. Straight, folded leaves 1–3 cm long x 1–3 mm wide, at right angles to stem and ending in a sharp point.

DEVIL'S PINS
Hovea pungens

DATE	PLACE

MAY–OCTOBER
VERY COMMON

Forest and woodland. Geraldton to Augusta, Cape Arid, Kojonup, Narrogin and Wongan Hills.
Shrub 10–70 cm high. Purple to blue pea flowers 10–20 mm across in spike 10–20 cm long at end of branch. Rough, straight or oval leaves 1–8 cm long x 2–35 mm wide, sometimes ending in a sharp point.

COMMON HOVEA
Hovea trisperma

DATE	PLACE

WILD VIOLET

Hybanthus calycinus

JULY–DECEMBER
VERY COMMON

Forest, woodland and heath in sand. Kalbarri to Margaret River, Bridgetown and Toodyay.
Herb 10–60 cm high. Blue to purple flowers 10–15 mm across on a stalk 10–20 cm long. Flat, straight leaves 1–4 cm long x 1–3 mm wide.

DATE	PLACE

BLUE LESCHENAULTIA

Lechenaultia biloba

AUGUST–DECEMBER
COMMON

Forest, woodland and heath in gravel and rock. Mullewa to Augusta, Esperance and Southern Cross.
Erect or straggly shrub 0.2–1 m high. Blue or white flowers 2–3 cm across in irregular clusters. Blunt, needle-like leaves 5–15 mm long x 1 mm wide.

DATE	PLACE

SLENDER LOBELIA
Lobelia tenuior

OCTOBER–JANUARY
VERY COMMON

Woodland, heath and edges of swamps in sand or gravel. Gingin to Lancelin, Augusta and Albany.
Slender plant 10–50 cm tall. Blue flowers, with ribs on bud, 1–2 cm across on stalks 7–15 cm long. Oval or straight, toothed or lobed leaves 2–7 cm long x 3–10 mm wide.

DATE	PLACE

PURPLE MAT RUSH
Lomandra purpurea

SEPTEMBER–DECEMBER
UNCOMMON

Woodland in sand or gravel. Mundaring to Perth, Augusta, Two Peoples Bay and Kojonup.
Herb 0.1–1.5 m high. Purple-black tubular flowers 5–10 mm long in closely-spaced rings around stem in spike 10–30 cm long on stalk 0.5–1.5 m long. Straight grass-like leaves 20–60 cm long x 5–10 mm wide, all at base of plant.

DATE	PLACE

MORNING IRIS

Orthrosanthus laxus

JULY–OCTOBER
COMMON

Forest, woodland and heath in sand or gravel. Kalbarri to Augusta, Albany, Kulin and Koorda.
Herb 15–60 cm high. Several blue flowers 3–4 cm across in a group on a stalk longer than the leaves. Flat, grass-like leaves 10–40 cm long x 1–5 mm wide, mostly at base of plant.

DATE	PLACE

RUSH-LEAVED PATERSONIA

Patersonia juncea

SEPTEMBER–NOVEMBER
UNCOMMON

Forest, woodland and heath in sand or gravel. Eneabba to Augusta, Cape Arid and Kulin.
Herb 10–40 cm high. Purple flowers 3–4 cm across in a head 3–4 cm long on a stalk 5–25 cm long. Straight, grass-like leaves 5–20 cm long x 0.5–1 mm wide, all at base of plant.

DATE	PLACE

AUGUST–JANUARY
UNCOMMON

BLUE PEPPER AND SALT

Philotheca nodiflora

Forest and woodland in gravel. Paynes Find to New Norcia, Busselton, Albany, Cape Le Grand and Wagin.
Shrub 10–80 cm high. Blue or pink flowers 5–15 mm across in a compact head 1–2 cm across, usually in the middle of a fork at or near the top of the branch. Smooth or hairy, blunt, needle-like leaves 5–15 mm long x 0.5–1 mm wide.

DATE	PLACE

JUNE–DECEMBER
COMMON

PLATYTHECA

Platytheca galioides

Forest, woodland and heath in damp areas. Jurien to Augusta, Bremer Bay, Jerramungup and Darkan.
Shrub 20–60 cm high with delicate stems. Drooping purple to blue flowers 10–20 mm across. Blunt, needle-like leaves 10–15 mm long x 0.5 mm wide in rings of eight around stem.

DATE	PLACE

PURPLE FAN

Scaevola calliptera

OCTOBER–MARCH
COMMON

Forest and woodland in sand or gravel. New Norcia to Perth, Augusta, Albany, Porongurup Range and Rocky Gully.

Prostrate shrub 10–40 cm high with spreading not upward-pointing hairs on stem. Blue to purple fan-shaped flowers 2–3 cm across. Hairy, toothed leaves, spoon-shaped (at base) or oval (along stem), 2–7 cm long x 5–25 mm wide.

DATE	PLACE

THICK-LEAVED FANFLOWER

Scaevola crassifolia

JULY–FEBRUARY
VERY COMMON

Coastal heath in sand. Karratha to Augusta, Albany and Eucla.

Shrub 0.1–1.5 m high. Blue, mauve or white flowers 10–15 mm across. Toothed circular, oval or spoon-shaped leaves 3–8 cm long x 1–3 cm wide.

DATE	PLACE

ALL YEAR
COMMON

AUSTRALIAN BLUEBELL

Sollya heterophylla

Woodland and heath. Mogumber to Perth, Augusta, Albany, Caiguna and Kulin. Twining shrub 0.5–5 m high. Hanging blue flowers 10 mm long x 10 mm wide. Spear-shaped or oval leaves 3–5 cm long x 5–20 mm wide.

DATE	PLACE

AUGUST–OCTOBER
VERY COMMON

PURPLE TASSELS

Sowerbaea laxiflora

Woodland and heath in sand or clay. Kalbarri to Augusta, Denmark and Narrogin. Herb 15–45 cm high. Purple flowers 10 mm across in a circular head 2–4 cm across at end of stalk 15–45 cm long. Straight, grass-like leaves 10–40 cm long x 1–2 mm wide, all at base of plant.

DATE	PLACE

BLIND GRASS

Stypandra glauca

JULY–NOVEMBER
VERY COMMON

Forest, woodland and heath on granite rocks or in clay or gravel. Kalbarri to Augusta, Cape Arid, Balladonia and Kalgoorlie.
Straggly herb 0.3–1 m high. Hanging blue flowers 10–15 mm across. Grass-like leaves 5–10 cm long x 1–5 mm wide along stem.

DATE	PLACE

QUEEN OF SHEBA

Thelymitra variegata

JUNE–SEPTEMBER
UNCOMMON

Woodland and heath. Dongara to Augusta, Albany, Esperance and Manjimup.
Slender plant 10–35 cm high. One to five purple, orange, red and yellow flowers 3–5 cm across scattered along stem. Spiral, grass-like leaf 5–10 cm long x 2–5 mm wide at base of plant.

DATE	PLACE

SEPTEMBER–NOVEMBER
UNCOMMON

BLUE LADY ORCHID

Thelymitra crinita

Forest and woodland. Jurien to Augusta, Albany, Esperance and Katanning.
Slender plant 20–70 cm high. Two to twenty blue flowers 3 cm across grouped at top of stem. Oval leaf 5–15 cm long x 1–3 cm wide at base of plant.

DATE	PLACE

AUGUST–NOVEMBER
COMMON

SCENTED SUN ORCHID

Thelymitra macrophylla

Forest, woodland and heath. Northampton, and Bindoon to Stirling Range, Esperance and Katanning.
Slender plant 30–50 cm high. Two to twenty sweetly scented blue flowers 3–4 cm across scattered along stem. Spear-shaped leaf 10–25 cm long x 2–5 cm wide at base of plant.

DATE	PLACE

MANY-FLOWERED FRINGE LILY

Thysanotus multiflorus

OCTOBER–DECEMBER
COMMON

Forest, woodland and heath in sand and gravel. Cataby to Augusta, Cape Le Grand, Manjimup and Toodyay.
Herb 10–70 cm high. Purple feathery-edged flowers 10–25 mm across in an umbrella shaped head 5–10 cm across at end of single stalk 15–70 cm long. Many smooth grass like leaves 10–60 cm long x 1–5 mm wide, all at base of plant.

DATE	PLACE

HOOKER'S BLADDERWORT

Utricularia inaequalis

OCTOBER–JANUARY
COMMON

Swamps. Bullsbrook to Perth, Busselton, Walpole, Cape Le Grand, Rocky Gully and Collie.
Herb 5–20 cm high. Single purple and yellow flower 10–20 mm long x 15–35 mm wide divided into three lobes at the end of a thin stalk 5–20 cm long. Thin, pointed leaves 1–3 cm long x 1 mm wide, all at base of plant.

List of multi-coloured wildflowers

Red flowers

Spiked Andersonia	20
Pink Rainbow	23
Common Mountain Bell	23
Swan River Myrtle	26
Tassel Flower	31
Rose Banjine	34
Water Bush	41
Common Brown Pea	41
Broad-leaved Brown Pea	42
Lemon-scented Darwinia	42
Heart-leaf Flame Pea	43
Yellow-eyed Flame Pea	43
Fire Bush	44
York Road Poison	47
Sandplain Poison	47
Golden-haired Pea	48
Holly Pea	48
Chittick	49
Bacon and Eggs	50
Common Catspaw	54
Albany Catspaw	54
Cowslip Orchid	56
Rattle Pea	59
Common Donkey Orchid	59
Beautiful Yellow Pea	60
Granny's Bonnet	64
Yellow Mountain Pea	65
Bushy Yellow Pea	65
Veined Yellow Pea	66
Silky Yellow Pea	66
Striped Bush Pea	70
Bristly Yellow Featherflower	72
Kick Bush	75
White Spider Orchid	77
Pearl Flower	79
White Cottonheads	79
Pom-Pom Darwinia	80
Rabbit Orchid	86
Common Woollybush	93
Jug Orchid	94
Queen of Sheba	110

Pink flowers

Rigid Cranberry	2
Firewood Banksia	3
Scarlet Flame Pea	9
Mouse Ears	10
Spindle Heath	13
Crinkle-leaved Poison	15
Nodding Banksia	39
Creeping Banksia	40
Heart-leaf Flame Pea	43
Yellow-eyed Flame Pea	43
Couch Honeypot	46
Holly-leaved Banksia	56
Plume Petrophile	68
Kick Bush	75
Camphor Myrtle	76
White Starflower	78
Many-flowered Smokebush	78
Pom-Pom Darwinia	80
Spindly Grevillea	83
Tassel Grevillea	84
Mayweed Sunray	85
White Myrtle	85
Woodbridge Poison	86
Pearly Beard-heath	87
White Banjine	88
Mountain Banjine	88
Forest Banjine	89
Reed Triggerplant	91
Hidden Featherflower	92
Common Woollybush	93
Posy Starflower	95
Blue Pepper and Salt	107
Thick-leaved Fanflower	108

Orange flowers

Basket Flower	1
Scarlet Banksia	3
Firewood Banksia	3
Scarlet Flame Pea	9
Toolbrunup Bell	13
Southern Rose	14
Crinkle-leaved Poison	15
Hairy Red Pea	18
Mountain Pea	18
Pincushion Triggerplant	37
Rattle Pea	59
Common Donkey Orchid	59
Prickly Dryandra	60
Beautiful Yellow Pea	60
Granny's Bonnet	64
Stinkwood	64
Bushy Yellow Pea	65
Veined Yellow Pea	66
Silky Yellow Pea	66
Striped Bush Pea	70
Common Velleia	72
Bristly Yellow Featherflower	72
Queen of Sheba	110

Brown flowers

Rusty Spider Orchid	7
Veined Yellow Pea	66
Striped Bush Pea	70
Common Velleia	72
Jug Orchid	94

Yellow flowers

Firewood Banksia	3
Common Dragon Orchid	6
Bee Orchid	7
Butterfly Orchid	8
King Spider Orchid	8
Crab-lipped Spider Orchid	9
Scarlet Flame Pea	9
Granite Rose	14
Scarlet Runner	16
Pincushion Triggerplant	37
Creeping Banksia	40
Water Bush	41
Common Brown Pea	41
Broad-leaved Brown Pea	42
Heart-leaf Flame Pea	43
Yellow-eyed Flame Pea	43
Fire Bush	44
King-in-his-Carriage	44
Dunsborough Donkey Orchid	45
Pansy Orchid	45
Showy Dryandra	46
Couch Honeypot	46
York Road Poison	47
Sandplain Poison	47
Golden-haired Pea	48
Holly Pea	48
Orange Stars	49
Chittick	49
Rattle Beaks	50
Bacon and Eggs	50
Christmas Tree	51
Leopard Orchid	52
Custard Orchid	52
Catkin Grevillea	84
Mayweed Sunray	85
Mountain Banjine	88
Cow Kicks	91
Common Woollybush	93
Queen of Sheba	110
Hooker's Bladderwort	112

White flowers

...igid Cranberry	2
...carlet Banksia	3
...Mondurup Bell	11
...ranbrook Bell	11
...Vittwers Mountain Bell	12
...airy Red Pea	18
...Mountain Pea	18
...lbany Daisy	19
...ink Fairies	19
...ticky Starflower	22
...Common Mountain Bell	23
...ink Rainbow	23
...rickly Hakea	25
...nakebush	25
...lat-topped Coneflower	27
...assel Flower	31
...Graceful Honeymyrtle	31
...epper and Salt	32
...ose-tipped Mulla Mulla	35
...ink Fountain Triggerplant	36
...ook Triggerplant	36
...incushion Triggerplant	37
...ern Heath	67
...lume Petrophile	68
...caly Petrophile	69
...ticky Petrophile	69
...ıg Orchid	94
...lue-tipped Smokebush	96
...lender Smokebush	97
...lue Leschenaultia	104
...hick-leaved Fanflower	108

Green/Black flowers

...Mangles Kangaroo Paw	2
...Common Dragon Orchid	6
...ee Orchid	7
...utterfly Orchid	8
...ing Spider Orchid	8
...rab-lipped Spider	9
...lat One-sided Bottlebrush	10
...ranbrook Bell	11
...outhern Rose	14
...Granite Rose	14
...ing-in-his-Carriage	44
...attle Beaks	50
...lying Duck Orchid	51
...lbany Catspaw	54
...Holly-leaved Banksia	56
...cented Banjine	70
...Native Wisteria	101
...urple Mat Rush	105

Blue/Purple flowers

Barrens Bottlebrush	4
Common Dragon Orchid	6
Mountain Pea	18
Foxtails	20
Spiked Andersonia	20
Bushy Boronia	21
Common Milkwort	22
Hairy Pink Pea	24
Snakebush	25
Silky Hemigenia	26
Hairy Kunzea	30
Curved-leaf Kunzea	30
Holly-leaved Mirbelia	32
Pepper and Salt	32
Karri Fanflower	35
Pink Fountain Triggerplant	36
Black-eyed Susan	38
Nodding Banksia	39
Stirling Range Banksia	40
Dunsborough Donkey Orchid	45
Pansy Orchid	45
Flying Duck Orchid	51
Many-flowered Smokebush	78
Pearl Flower	79
White Cottonheads	79
Blue Devils	81
Woodbridge Poison	86
Felted Swamp Flower	90

116

Index

Acacia pulchella	53	
saligna	53	
Actinodium calocephalum	19	
Actinotus leucocephalus	73	
Adenanthos barbiger	1	
cygnorum	93	
obovatus	1	
Agonis flexuosa	73	
Andersonia Giant	74	
Spiked	20	
Spiny	74	
Andersonia axilliflora	74	
caerulea	20	
echinocephala	74	
simplex	20	
Anigozanthos humilis	54	
manglesii subsp. manglesii	2	
preissii	54	
Anthocercis viscosa	75	
Astroloma epacridis	2	
pallidum	75	
Bacon and Eggs	50	
Baeckea camphorosmae	76	
Banjine Coastal	34	
Forest	89	
Mountain	88	
Rose	34	
Scented	70	
White	88	
Banksia Bull	55	
Creeping	40	
Firewood	3	
Holly-leaved	56	
Nodding	39	
Prostrate	39	
Scarlet	3	
Slender	55	
Stirling Range	40	
Banksia attenuata	55	
coccinea	3	
gardneri	39	
grandis	55	
ilicifolia	56	
menziesii	3	
nutans	39	
repens	40	
solandri	40	

Basket Flower	1	
Beard-heath Pearly	87	
Beaufortia anisandra	4	
cyrtodonta	4	
incana	5	
Bell Common Mountain	23	
Cranbrook	11	
Gillam's	12	
Mondurup	11	
Toolbrunup	13	
Wittwers Mountain	12	
Yellow Mountain	58	
Black-Eyed Susan	38	
Bladderwort Hooker's	112	
Blind Grass	110	
Blue Devils	81	
Squill	95	
Bluebell Australian	109	
Boronia Bushy	21	
Pink	21	
Boronia fastigiata	21	
pulchella	21	
Borya sphaerocephala	76	
Bossiaea aquifolium	41	
eriocarpa	41	
ornata	42	
Bottlebrush Albany	5	
Barrens	4	
Flat One-sided	10	
Grey-leaved	5	
Stirling Range	4	
Burchardia umbellata	77	
Buttercup Common	71	
Yellow	62	
Caladenia arenicola	6	
barbarossa	6	
discoidea	7	
ferruginea	7	
flava	56	
latifolia	19	
lobata	8	
longicauda subsp. longicauda	77	
pectinata	8	
plicata	9	
Callistemon glaucus	5	
Calothamnus rupestris	10	
torulosus	10	

alytrix glutinosa 22
    leschenaultii 95
    tetragona 78
amphor Myrtle 76
atspaw Albany 54
    Common 54
hamaescilla corymbosa 95
hittick 49
horizema cordatum 43
    dicksonii 43
    rhombeum 9
hristmas Tree 51
omesperma virgatum 22
oneflower Flat-topped 27
    Magnificent 29
    Pincushion 28
    Rose 28
    Spoon-leaved 63
    Stirling Range 27
onospermum coerulescens subsp. *dorrienii* 96
    floribundum 78
    huegelii 97
    spectabile 96
onostephium pendulum 79
onostylis candicans 57
    juncea 57
    pusilla 58
    setosa 79
osmelia rubra 13
ottonheads Grey 57
    Rush 57
    Silvery 58
    White 79
ouch Honeypot 46
ow Kicks 91
anberry Rigid 2
anicula gemmata 98
    sericea 98

aisy Albany 19
ampiera Angled-stem 100
    Common 99
    Karri 100
    Winged-stem 99
ampiera alata 99
    hederacea 100
    linearis 99
    trigona 100
arwinia Lemon-scented 42
    Pom-Pom 80
arwinia citriodora 42
    collina 58
    hypericifolia 13
    lejostyla 23

Darwinia macrostegia 11
    meeboldii 11
    oxylepis 12
    vestita 80
    wittwerorum 12
Dasypogon bromeliifolius 80
Daviesia oppositifolia 59
    physodes 44
Devil's Pins 103
Dianella revoluta 97
Diplolaena dampieri 14
    graniticola 14
Diuris aff.*amplissima* 45
    corymbosa 59
    magnifica 45
Drakaea glyptodon 44
Drosera menziesii 23
    stolonifera subsp. *porrecta* 81
Dryandra Prickly 60
    Showy 46
Dryandra falcata 60
    formosa 46
    lindleyana 46

Elythranthera brunonis 101
    emarginata 24
Eryngium pinnatifidum 81
Eucalyptus marginata 82
Eutaxia densifolia 60

Fanflower Karri 35
    Thick-leaved 108
Featherflower Bristly Yellow 72
    Hidden 92
Fern Heath 67
Fire Bush 44
Flag Yellow 68
Flame Pea Heart-leaf 43
    Scarlet 9
    Yellow-eyed 43
Flannel Flower 73
Foxtails 20

Gastrolobium calycinum 47
    microcarpum 47
    villosum 15
Gompholobium tomentosum 63
    villosum 24
Granny's Bonnet 64
Grevillea Catkin 84
    Spindly 83
    Tassel 84
    Wilson's 15
    Woolly-flowered 83

Grevillea endlicheriana	83	King-in-his-Carriage	44
pilulifera	83	Kunzea Curved-Leaf	3C
synapheae	84	Hairy	3C
tenuiflora	84	Kunzea preissiana	3C
wilsonii	15	recurva	3C
Guinea Flower Golden	61	Lambertia inermis	49
Long-leaved	62	Lechenaultia biloba	104
		Leptoceras menziesii	86
Hairy Jug Flower	1	Leschenaultia Blue	104
Hakea Prickly	25	Leucopogon strictus	87
White-veined	82	verticillatus	31
Hakea ambigua	82	Lily Blueberry	29
amplexicaulis	25	Hooded Pink	97
Hardenbergia comptoniana	101	Many-flowered Fringe	112
Hemiandra pungens	25	Lobelia Slender	105
Hemigenia Silky	26	Lobelia tenuior	10.
Hemigenia incana	26	Lomandra nigricans	87
Hibbertia Cutleaf	61	purpurea	105
Hibbertia aurea	61	Lyperanthus serratus	56
cuneiformis	61		
huegelii	62	Macrozamia riedlei	97
hypericoides	62	Marianthus Red	16
stellaris	49	Marianthus erubescens	16
Honeymyrtle Graceful	31	Mat Rush Dark	87
Hovea Common	103	Purple	105
Holly-leaved	102	Melaleuca lateritia	1
Tree	102	radula	3
Hovea chorizemifolia	102	Mesomelaena tetragona	6
elliptica	102	Milkmaids	7
pungens	103	Milkwort Common	2
trisperma	103	Mirbelia Holly-leaved	3
Hyalosperma cotula	85	Mirbelia dilatata	3
Hybanthus calycinus	104	Mouse Ears	1
Hypocalymma angustifolium	85	Mulla Mulla Rose-tipped	3
robustum	26	Myrtle Swan River	2
		White	8
Iris Morning	106		
Isopogon asper	27	Native Wisteria	10
attenuatus	63	Nemcia capitata	56
baxteri	27	crenulata	6
dubius	28	leakeana	1
formosus	28	pulchella	6
latifolius	29	reticulata	6
Isotoma hypocrateriformis	86	retusa	6
Isotropis cuneifolia	64	rubra	1
		Nuytsia floribunda	5
Jacksonia calycina	48		
densiflora	48	Oligarrhena micrantha	6
sternbergiana	64	Orange Stars	4
Jarrah	82	Orchid Bee	
Johnsonia teretifolia	29	Bird	9
		Blue China	9
Kangaroo Paw Mangles	2	Blue Lady	11
Kennedia prostrata	16	Butterfly	
Kick Bush	75	Carousel Spider	

Orchid Common Donkey	59
Common Dragon	6
Cowslip	56
Crab-lipped Spider	9
Custard	52
Dunsborough Donkey	45
Flying Duck	51
Hooded Leek	89
Jug	94
King Spider	8
Leopard	52
Pansy	45
Pink Enamel	24
Purple Enamel	101
Rabbit	86
Rusty Spider	7
Scented Sun	111
Silky Blue	98
White Spider	77
Orthrosanthus laxus	106
Paper-heath Stirling Range	90
Paracaleana nigrita	51
Patersonia Rush-leaved	106
Patersonia juncea	106
umbrosa var. *xanthina*	68
Pea Beautiful Yellow	60
Broad-leaved Brown	42
Bushy Yellow	65
Common Brown	41
Golden-haired	48
Hairy Pink	24
Hairy Red	18
Hairy Yellow	63
Holly	48
Mountain	18
Rattle	59
Silky Yellow	66
Striped Bush	70
Veined Yellow	66
Yellow Mountain	65
Pearl Flower	79
Pepper and Salt	32
Blue	107
Peppermint	73
Petrophile Granite	33
Plume	68
Scaly	69
Sticky	69
Petrophile biloba	33
linearis	33
serruriae	68
squamata	69
striata	69
Philotheca nodiflora	107
spicata	32
Pimelea ciliata	88
ferruginea	34
lehmanniana	88
rosea	34
suaveolens	70
sylvestris	89
Pincushions	76
Pineapple Bush	80
Pink Fairies	19
Petticoats	38
Rainbow	23
Pixie Mops	33
Platytheca galioides	107
Platytheca	107
Poison Crinkle-leaved	15
Sandplain	47
Woodbridge	86
York Road	47
Prasophyllum cucullatum	89
Prickly Moses	53
Pterostylis barbata	94
recurva	94
Ptilotus manglesii	35
Pultenaea strobilifera	70
Purple Fan	108
Tassels	109
Pyrorchis nigricans	17
Queen of Sheba	110
Ranunculus colonorum	71
Rattle Beaks	50
Red Beaks	17
Robin Redbreast Bush	17
Rose Granite	14
Southern	14
Scaevola auriculata	35
calliptera	108
crassifolia	108
Scarlet Runner	16
Sedge Semaphore	67
Smokebush Blue-tipped	96
Many-flowered	78
Slender	97
Stirling Range	96
Snakebush	25
Sollya heterophylla	109
Southern Cross	92
Sowerbaea laxiflora	109
Sphenotoma sp.	90
Spindle Heath	13

Starflower Posy	95
Sticky	22
White	78
Sticky Tailflower	75
Stinkwood	64
Stylidium brunonianum	36
calcaratum	36
junceum	91
scandens	37
schoenoides	91
uniflorum	37
Stypandra glauca	110
Sundew Leafy	81
Sunray Mayweed	85
Swamp Flower Felted	90
Synaphea Granite	71
Synaphea acutiloba	71
Tassel Flower	31
Tetratheca hirsuta	38
Thelymitra benthamiana	52
crinita	111
macrophylla	111
variegata	110
villosa	52

Thysanotus multiflorus	112
Tribonanthes australis	90
Triggerplant Book	36
Climbing	37
Pincushion	37
Pink Fountain	36
Reed	91
Utricularia inaequalis	112
multifida	38
Velleia Common	72
Velleia trinervis	72
Verticordia acerosa	72
habrantha	92
Water Bush	41
Wattle Orange	53
Wild Violet	104
Wollybush Common	93
Xanthosia rotundifolia	92
Zamia	93

Selected Reading

Bennett, E.M. *Common and Aboriginal Names of Western Australian Plant Species.* 2nd Edition. Glen Forrest: Wildflower Society of Western Australia (1991).

Blackall, W.E., and Grieve, B.J. *How to Know Western Australian Wildflowers.* Parts 1-4. Nedlands: University of Western Australia Press (1954-1982).

Corrick, M.G., Fuhrer, B.A., and George, A.S. *Wildflowers of Southern Western Australia.* Noble Park, Victoria: Five Mile Press (1996).

Erickson, R., George, A.S., Marchant, N.G., and Morcombe, M.K. *Flowers and Plants of Western Australia.* Sydney: Reed (1973).

Grieve, B.J. *How to Know Western Australian Wildflowers.* Part 2. 2nd Edition. Nedlands: University of Western Australia Press (1998).

Hoffman, N., and Brown, A. *Orchids of South-West Australia.* Revised 2nd Edition. Nedlands: University of Western Australia Press (1998).

Marchant, N.G., Wheeler, J.R., Rye, B.L., Bennett, E.M., Lander, N.S., and Macfarlane, T.D. *Flora of the Perth Region.* Perth: Western Australian Herbarium (1987).

Nevill, S., and McQuoid, N. *Guide to the Wildflowers of South Western Australia.* Perth: Simon Nevill Publications (1998).